STOLEN HONOR

STOLEN HONOR

FALSELY ACCUSED, IMPRISONED, AND MY LONG ROAD TO FREEDOM

CLINT LORANCE

CENTER
STREET®

NEW YORK NASHVILLE

Center Street
Hachette Book Group
1290 Avenue of the Americas, New York, NY 10104
centerstreet.com
twitter.com/centerstreet

First Edition: September 2020

Center Street is a division of Hachette Book Group, Inc. The Center Street name and logo are trademarks of Hachette Book Group, Inc.

The publisher is not responsible for websites (or their content) that are not owned by the publisher.

The Hachette Speakers Bureau provides a wide range of authors for speaking events. To find out more, go to www.HachetteSpeakersBureau.com or call (866) 376-6591.

Library of Congress Cataloging-in-Publication Data has been applied for.

ISBNs: 978-1-5460-5959-2 (hardcover), 978-1-5460-5961-5 (ebook)

Printed in the United States of America

LSC-C

10 9 8 7 6 5 4 3 2 1

CONTENTS

CONTENTS

Waste no more time arguing what a
good man should be. Be one.

—MARCUS AURELIUS

If thou faint in the day of adversity,
thy strength is small.

—PROVERBS 24:10

STOLEN HONOR

INTRODUCTION

WORD SPREAD LIKE WILDFIRE through the prison at Fort Leavenworth on that Friday before Memorial Day in May 2019. Several news outlets were reporting that President Trump was considering pardons for unspecified military servicemen who had been labeled war criminals by *The New York Times*. The reports suggested the pardons would be issued on Memorial Day, four days hence. My name was mentioned as one of the top candidates for a pardon.

I was six years into a 20-year sentence for my role

1

in the deaths of two Taliban insurgents in Afghanistan in 2012 who were posing a deadly threat to the soldiers under my command. Many of the military prisoners in Leavenworth had become strong supporters in my celebrated case as an Army officer betrayed by his superiors. Word that a pardon was at my doorstep set off great celebratory anticipation at the prison and among the thousands who had rallied to my cause.

I had traveled a long road from North Texas to the Army and on to Korea and Iraq and then, as a paratrooper with the 82nd Airborne, into the Taliban-infested regions of southern Afghanistan. My military dress blues were well decorated with medals for my performance, and I took great pride in my rank as a first lieutenant.

But things went terribly wrong for me on a sweltering July day in the Kandahar region, where Taliban insurgents were highly active with their murderous activities against all that represented the United States. On that day, two motorcycle-riding insurgents—both with links to other deadly incidents—charged my platoon and were killed by men under my command, acting on my order.

I was relieved of my command and, after a long

delay, charged with two counts of second-degree murder of Afghan "civilians." At my court-martial, I was convicted and sentenced to 20 years in prison—a sentence later reduced to 19 years. I was 28 years old.

Surrounding the incident in Kandahar, as well as my prosecution and conviction, was a perfect storm of competing political forces. Not the least of these was the top-down notion in the Obama administration that our on-the-ground military forces should be constrained to use "proportional force" in facing our enemies in combat.

Now, to me, such thinking is not only irresponsible but highly dispiriting to the soldiers engaged in warfare on the ground. But that thinking trickled down from the White House and eventually carried the day with many of my superiors. It was this sort of thinking that paved the way to my sitting in prison in 2019 with 13 more years to serve.

A great groundswell of support had developed for my case, thanks to groups like United American Patriots and the Congressional Justice for Warriors Caucus. The only way out of my terrible situation was a pardon from the president, something that would never happen under President Obama. Still, my supporters presented Obama with a petition signed by 124,966 Americans. Obama's people sniffed and sent it to the Justice Department's pardon attorney for disposal.

But now, with Donald J. Trump in the White House, there was fresh hope in our hearts as we absorbed the news reports that he was going to act on Memorial Day. My supporters and I were sure the president would not let us down, and that weekend was filled with excitement.

But, alas, it was not to be—at least not yet.

PART I

MY FIRST LIFE

MY FAMILY MOVED A LOT when I was growing up in Texas and Oklahoma. During the years I was in school, the average length of time we stayed in the same place was 11 months. This meant that my brother and I were never able to settle into sports teams or clubs or anything that required a steady commitment. Our father was a successful and sought-after welder, and we moved wherever he could find the best jobs for his skills. My mom took care of finding suitable churches for us wherever we were living.

Because of our nomadic lifestyle, my family had a decided lack of interest in civic affairs. I doubt if my mom or dad could name their congressman or governor. They might have known the president's name, but they probably did not know the names of their senators. They definitely didn't know the names of mayors and county commissioners.

We didn't get involved with that kind of stuff because my family looked at that as rich people's responsibility. It was the job of people who were better than us to handle all that. Our job was to survive and feed our family. I remember reading about civics in school and thinking to myself, *I'm just some poor kid and my concern is making some money to buy the family a loaf of bread. I don't have the luxury to worry about who is going to be the president.*

I didn't plan on going into the military; I had always wanted to be a state trooper. State troopers were the most respectable people you could run into in my world. Everybody loved them, everybody was scared of them, nobody wanted to get a ticket. Put simply, my family always had the utmost reverence for police officers, back in a time when they all shined their boots or shoes. They had impeccably pressed uniforms and were the most professional people you would ever meet. We didn't interact with many military service members, but we had cops in our family, and we had a cop in our church, so I was exposed to them. And I liked them.

People are influenced by media more than they like to admit. When I was young, I recall my siblings and me watching a movie where somebody was being held hostage. Dramatic music played as the criminals prepared to kill the guy. Then all of a sudden, police cars swarmed the building and the cops burst through the door to save the hostage at the last second. Everyone in the room cheered. I took a lot of cues from that. The lesson was simple: police protect people. I liked that. At one point during high school, I became a member of the junior police explorers, and I loved it. If I could have become a cop at the age of 16, I would've done just that.

We were living in a small town in Oklahoma when, on April 19, 1995, a terrorist blew up the federal building in Oklahoma City, killing 168 innocent men, women, and children. Over 500 others were injured in the blast. I was in fourth grade, and Mrs. Bingham, our teacher, brought in a small television set so we could watch the coverage. We all wept at the horror unfolding before us. It was my first experience in trying to comprehend such profound evil. My great grandmother, watching the news, had a severe stroke. For the rest of her life, she mumbled, "All those babies."

But that devastating event was only a forerunner of what was to come.

On September 11, 2001, I was almost 17 years old and living in one of the endless suburbs of Dallas. I always needed to earn money and was fortunate that my high school had a work-release program that allowed me to leave in the afternoon in order to get extra work hours. I had three jobs at the time. Monday through Friday, I'd leave school at 1:45 pm and drive to the Farmersville Texaco to clean the station as a maintenance worker. At 2:30 pm, I'd change into a Tom Thumb uniform in the gas station bathroom and drive to the Tom Thumb grocery store in McKinney to work until 11 pm. On Saturdays and Sundays, I worked all-day shifts at Feagin's Supermarket in Farmersville.

On the morning of September 11, I was stopping to cash a check at Feagin's. I walked in and saw Kathy, one of the owners, staring at a small television. That was the first sign something was wrong. She had this little tiny black-and-white television set that she kept up in the front office of the store. I knew she hid it up there;

she never wanted anybody to see that she was watching TV. That day, though, she had it on the counter and a handful of customers were gathered around it, their faces wet with tears.

"Kathy, what are you doing?" I asked. When I saw that she was crying, I knew something must be terribly wrong. I had known Kathy for a long time. She's a strong, proud Southern woman. She doesn't cry easily.

There was hysteria on the television; nobody knew what was going on. The reporters were saying all kinds of dramatic stuff about the United States being under attack and that more attacks were coming. I looked around the store at the grittiest, strongest people I knew, and this had brought them to their knees.

Watching that little TV, clenching my jaw, it suddenly came to me: "I've got to do something, but what can a 17-year-old boy do?"

Soon enough, I went to the Army recruiting station in Greenville, Texas, right across from Walmart—a place where you could get a gallon of milk, get your tires changed, and join the Army. The recruiter said that since I had my GED, what I needed were 12 college credits. I told him that I could have that, through a community college, by the end of the year. "Okay, come back on your birthday or at the end of the semester," he said. It all worked out since I turned 18 that December.

I knew that I had to get my act together in terms of my finances, too. When I was 16, I convinced my mom to co-sign a loan for me, and I got a Ford Ranger. She signed under one condition: I would have to get a manual transmission as my first vehicle. Learn the most difficult first, she believed, and then everything else is easy. My goal was always to pay off the Ranger before I turned 18. But now this goal was even more pressing since I wanted to join the Army without leaving any loose ends behind.

When I started attending a community college in August, my dad offered to pay for my classes, but I told him that I already had the money.

Dad's offer to pay was unexpected. In my family, there was no expectation that the family would pay for a child's education. The expectation was that you leave the house when you're 18 years old, you have your own job, you have your own truck, you have your own independence. You never want to involve someone else in your problems.

My family tree doesn't include many military

veterans. My father's father served. He died of heart disease before I was born, so I never met him.

I never got the opportunity to talk to my grandfather or to my grandmother. Even if it's just a story that he joined the Army to get a job, it says something about my family that we retell it. But my family very much loves this country. I'm not sure if they know why they do or why they believe this country is better than other countries, but they are patriots for sure.

I didn't have much exposure to the military when I was a kid, but it was still the most highly revered institution in all the communities where I lived. Anybody who wore the uniform in those areas of Oklahoma and Texas was going to be treated as royalty. And I noticed.

When I was a little kid, one of my cousins joined the Army. He came home wearing a uniform, the old green camouflage, and he wore it well. He took pride in it. He did a great job representing the uniform. I remember being so proud of him and thinking, *I want to be like that someday.* I thought it was just so cool.

I'll say this: now, it's going to be even more rare for anyone in my family to want to join the military. Several of my nephews and nieces have talked about joining, but our family basically riots. They say, "Oh no, you're not. Not after what happened to Clint." But that's getting ahead of my story.

In December, I moved in with my aunt Jean in Texas and focused on getting all my stuff together and my affairs in order. My mom was looking to move back to Oklahoma. I told her I was staying in Texas with Aunt Jean and Uncle Brian. My mother told me that she understood. I paid off my truck and joined the Army on my 18th birthday.

On April 15, 2003, Aunt Jean and my cousin Jamie took me to a hotel in Dallas. We went to an IMAX movie after we checked in. It was something silly with talking animals. I was so stressed out that I didn't pay much attention. I was going to start my Army career the next morning.

Aunt Jean went all out and brought all kinds of food back to the hotel. We just sat there and gorged on Burger King and pizza and cried and laughed all night. The next morning at 3 am, Aunt Jean dropped me off at a huge hotel in Dallas. The military had rented the whole conference room area. There were hundreds of us, new recruits joining all branches of the military.

It was all very orderly and controlled by non-- commissioned officers (NCOs) from the Army, the

Coast Guard, and the other military branches. There was never a question about what was going on. I loved that quality of organization. I really appreciated that, from the very beginning.

There were a bunch of chartered buses at the loading docks, out back with the dumpsters. These buses took us to the Dallas/Fort Worth Airport, where a special part of the terminal was reserved for the military. Everything happened right on cue. There were no hiccups, no questions or confusion about what was happening. I said to myself, *I'm going to love this organization.*

Wheels up, and we were off to Chicago's O'Hare, where we then boarded a very small plane that flew us to St. Louis. From there, the drill sergeants collected us and bused us on to Fort Leonard Wood in Missouri. And that's where the serious basic training began.

2003

I had no idea what to expect as we pulled up to the 43rd Reception Battalion at Fort Leonard Wood. In the Army, every time you change duty stations, the first place you go is to a reception battalion. They process arrivals, acclimate them to their new station, and make sure everything's squared away.

The buses pulled to a stop and the kids started to pour out. The drill sergeants lined up to establish a gauntlet right outside the doors. There were dozens of sergeants out there, directing people to do all kinds of stuff. The main focus was on getting all the luggage in a perfect line. I thought, *Wow, this is cool. Everything's in order and structured, and I love it.*

We saw all this happen through the seat windows, even though we were supposed to be looking straight ahead, as the drill sergeant on our bus demanded.

Finally, it was our turn. A short female drill sergeant leapt on board and started ordering us in high-pitched voice. "All right, privates, this is what you're going to do," she demanded. "You're going to get off. You're not going to waste anybody's time. You're not going to trip and fall. You're going to watch your feet. Anything you say from this point forward will be 'Yes, Drill Sergeant' or 'No, Drill Sergeant.'"

She gave us these commands quickly. "In the Army, we do things orderly, so you're not just all going to get up and start moving. You're going to move out from the front to the back. When we begin, the people in front of you will get up and start moving out, and then you'll get up. Everybody else will stay seated until it's their turn."

Now whenever I'm on an airplane, I always think, *I wish these people would just do things like the military so we can get out of here faster.* Another thing I still do when I get on an airplane is to put my backpack, if I have one on, on my front. That way I can sit right down in my seat and not get in people's way and hold up traffic. That's something that they teach you in the Army: efficiency.

We got off the bus and followed the drill sergeant's commands: "Don't look at me. Look straight forward. Get your head up. Don't look at the ground. Have confidence." During the process, I realized that what we were being taught was all the stuff that my grandpa had drilled into me: to have self-confidence and to treat every single human being with respect as if he or she was the most important person on earth.

The next couple of weeks in the reception battalion were occupied with assessments and preparation for Basic Training. A physical training (PT) test is done immediately to determine everybody's fitness level.

There are all these raw civilian recruits of all different athletic abilities. Each company has a couple hundred people, and they have to be careful how they separate everyone. If they assign people randomly, you could potentially end up with a company of 200 studs, or you could end up with a company of 200 duds. They have to mix it up to make sure that the duds get brought up to the stud level.

The Army controls everything you eat. Some of the new recruits are fat, so they put them on a nutrition plan, and they lose weight quickly. Some recruits have to stay in the reception battalion a lot longer than others.

In training, I learned that I liked to run. I didn't know that before because I was never exposed to running. We moved around so much when I was a kid that I couldn't join any athletic teams. Once we started running in training, I found that I really liked it. You don't have to be athletic. You just pick an end point and say, "I'm going to get to that point at this speed. Execute."

It's like everything else in life; you set a goal and you reach it.

The Marine Corps puts a lot of pressure on its recruits to lift weights and have a lot of upper body strength. The Army, on the other hand, focuses on endurance. This lines up with the services' different missions. The Marine Corps is designed to come in hard and fast, carrying what they need on their backs because they don't know when they're going to get more supplies. The Marines beat down the enemy and then hand the situation over to the Army to stay for a while. Soldiers travel long distances and stay. That's the way we fight, and we train like that. In the Army, you run and run and run.

I can't speak for the rest of the services, but in the Army at least, there's a culture of never accepting your best, of understanding that you can always do better. No matter what you're doing, you strive to do it more efficiently and faster.

I made some lifelong friends during my first months in the Army. We came from varied backgrounds. Alex Rosa was a Brooklyn native and a serious Mets fan. He was a tall, muscular guy with an Irish and Puerto Rican background. His father was murdered when he was an infant. He had a scar through his right eyebrow that he got when he was a kid. Alex was a personable guy, goofy but also a high-speed soldier. It was easy to like him.

Justin Lyle, from Washington State, was not an

overachiever. He was a mediocre soldier, so I did not like that about him. But I did like his intelligence and the fact he has a good heart. And he also seemed very loyal. Over time, he's proven that loyalty is at the root of his character.

Nancy Yacobucci was just like me. She grew up in a really poor family under terrible circumstances. Yacobucci is a tiny woman, maybe a hundred pounds soaking wet. The drill sergeants gave her a hard time about her size in Basic Training. They forced her to eat double what everybody else ate. I remember her saying at one point, "Drill Sergeant, I can't eat anymore!" About 15 of them just went for her, screaming, "Don't tell me you can't do something! You are in the Army! You can do anything you want! Now get over there and eat that cheesecake!"

It took 17 weeks to finish training at Fort Leonard Wood. These first steps were making us soldiers or, as the Army puts it, instilling "the Army's Values and Command Philosophy into Soldiers' everyday life." Basic Training included work with rifles, hand grenades, and nuclear, chemical, and biological protective gear.

After Basic Training came the Advanced Individual Training (AIT) that would make us military police (MPs). There's a slew of skills to master, including advanced map reading and qualifying on everything from pistols like the M9 to crew-served weapons like the M2 .50 cal. We learned defensive tactics and techniques, detainee operations, and battlefield forensics.

Toward the end of Basic Training, the drill sergeants came in with a bunch of forms and, as usual, a gruff set of orders. "Fill these out. These are the top three assignments that you want and you're not guaranteed to get any of them," they told us. I listed Germany, Korea, and Japan, all important places for the Army. I wanted to see more of the world but knew better than to get my hopes too high. "The chain of command is telling us we have to let you choose, but don't get a big head," the drill sergeants would say. "You privates don't have any control over anything." As if to prove it, my top choice of Germany soon got denied.

On a Saturday, a week before the end of AIT, a bunch of us walked over to the library on post and logged into our Army Knowledge Online (AKO) accounts. These were our new official email accounts, and getting one set up was part of our training.

There in my AKO account were my orders. I was going to Korea, and I was very excited to see that. Of course, we all immediately began comparing assignments. It's not like you can change your assignment, but you want to see who's going with you. At that point, you *know* that you're the low man on the totem pole in the Army and you don't want to go by yourself.

Luckily, I wasn't going alone. Rosa, Lyle, and Yacobucci were all assigned to Korea as well. We printed off our orders and took them back to our drill sergeants to inform them of our assignments.

My family came to my Basic Training graduation. My family was not accustomed to military graduations. They did not know what was expected of them, but they knew that they were proud to have a soldier in the family, so they put together a convoy of vehicles from Texas and Oklahoma, and they all drove to Missouri to watch me graduate and become a soldier in the World's Greatest Army. It wasn't just a momentous achievement for me; it was a milestone for us all—for my family and my entire community.

I rode home with them back to Texas and then reported to the Dallas/Fort Worth Airport for my first assignment. Of course, the Army gives you plane tickets. They flew me to Seattle, the meeting point to go to Korea.

PINPOINT ORDERS

I knew that I was going to be an MP in the Army and that I would be stationed somewhere in Korea, but I didn't know exactly where. The Army keeps those details from enlisted soldiers for security reasons until they get in-country.

Once in South Korea, our first stop was the personnel command headquarters where hundreds of other servicemen and women of all different ranks assembled in a huge formation. Officers came out and started yelling everybody's name and rank. When they yelled my name, I ran up and grabbed my paper from them, the paper containing my "pinpoint orders" telling me where I was headed.

I looked at the orders. I would be heading to Busan, South Korea's second-biggest city. Soon enough I learned I would have company—my recent acquaintances Justin Lyle, Alex Rosa, and Nancy Yacobucci.

We scouted around for directions for our next move and soon heard NCOs stalking around yelling, "If you're going to Busan, come over here!" They then put us on small buses that took us to the train station. We saw a handful of people we had been in Basic Training with on the bus, including a woman who later went AWOL and lived in Canada for several years.

The NCOs gave us specific directions, preparing us for the first time we were to be without NCOs since the start of the trip. "Okay, this is what you're going to do," one said. "You're going to go to this platform, get on this train. Do not get off until you get to Busan. When you get to Busan, go to the military liaison that's in the train station and check in with them. They'll tell you what to do from there."

I remember riding on the train with Nancy, Alex, and Justin. We all sat together and had a good time. When I would get up to go to the bathroom, I'd keep hitting my head and everybody would laugh.

We got out at the Busan train station and met the NCO there. Of course, he was being a hard nose. As a handful of brand-new privates, we were easy targets. He called somebody, and next thing I know another sergeant came in and said, "Okay, come with us."

There was a van waiting. We got in and the sergeant drove us through the heart of downtown Busan. That's when we got our first good look at Korea. I was overwhelmed by how big the city was and how many people there were everywhere, nothing like rural Oklahoma or the suburban sprawl of North Texas.

Korea, even in 2003, was light-years beyond anything you might see in the United States. It was so technologically advanced and immaculate—like something from *Star Trek*. There were all these little kids walking around talking on cell phones. The cool thing was that all the kids were wearing uniforms. It was neat, a lot more orderly than the United States. I remember thinking, *Wow, on this, the United States is kind of behind the power curve.*

When we reached our base, I saw a little post with a brown sign emblazoned with the U.S. Army seal and Camp Hialeah, spelled exactly like the city in Florida.

We arrived late at night, but the sergeants were ready for us. That's when I met my NCO, Staff Sergeant Scott VanValkenburg, who would soon change the trajectory of my Army career.

"Okay, Lorance," he said. "You're coming with me. Yacobucci, you're going over there; Lyle, over there." This was the first time our group from Basic got split up. We all went to different platoons, but at least we were all in the same company. We saw each other every day.

That first day, VanValkenburg told me, "You *will* go to college. You will be a PT stud. You will go to the Soldier of the Month board. You will do correspondence courses." Of course, he's telling me this as I'm in the pushup position. That's just how the Army is.

Early on in their careers, new soldiers are assessed in terms of their commitment to success. Which soldiers care about succeeding, and which don't care that much and just want to get through with the least effort? I was blessed with great leaders in my first days in the Army. Sergeant First Class Jenna Holman and Staff Sergeant Scott VanValkenburg did not give me a choice: I would be on the fast track. There's high turnover in Korea because it's only a year-long tour for most soldiers. I just happened to fall into the right place at the right time: they needed somebody to be their prize fighter, and they made me into that person immediately.

My superiors didn't give me a chance to even think about it. I just followed their lead. And it suited me. Everything they were saying made sense to me and fell in line with what I wanted to do with my life. I'll always have SFC Jenna Holman and SSG Van-Valkenburg to thank for steering me toward a successful career.

On top of a new post and a new career goal, as well as serving in a new country, there were new people to get used to. My first roommate was mixed-race, but he let me know immediately that he considered himself black. He hails from Chicago and he would let you know that quickly, too.

He was the absolute diametric opposite from what I was used to. It was absolutely a shock. We got into arguments about all kinds of stuff. But he opened my eyes to a lot of stuff, too. I'm glad I met him.

My second roommate was a Korean national, an augmentee to the U.S. Army. Most people aren't familiar with the Korean Augmentee to the United States Army (KATUSA) program. Because there is compulsory military service in Korea, rich Korean kids are able to serve in American units after they go to college. They live with us, work with us, and do everything except get paid by the United States. It's a very integrated program, but the augmentees wear a Korean flag on their shoulder instead of an American one.

My Korean roommate barely spoke any English, but we were able to learn from one another. He and all of his friends were always taking me off post somewhere. You would think that Americans would go overseas and say, "Wow, I want to open my eyes so that I'll see everything. I want to go do something new every day." But they don't. They stay on base, go to Pizza Hut, and rent American movies from the PX. They become insular. I was the opposite of that. I would find other like-minded soldiers and we would go off and explore.

Growing up, I'd always worn Wranglers, overalls, and farm and ranch clothes. I now found myself, at the age of 18, in a country with no real drinking age. One night when we were going out to a club, one my friends, a short Mexican-American woman from Arizona named Vivianna Vargas, pointed out the absurdity of what I was wearing. "You're not wearing that, are you?" she asked incredulously. "*Dios mio!* We're going shopping tomorrow." Four or five of us went out shopping after that, and they helped me buy normal people's clothes.

At first, being in a strange new country was a culture shock for me. But once my eyes began opening to the rest of the world, I wanted to see everything. I wanted to take it all in, every bit of it.

Some things I saw closer to post blew my mind. I never imagined how permissive or promiscuous people could be. A bunch of 18-year-old kids in a foreign country—you can use your imagination. I never thought respectable, professional people would act in such a questionable way in their personal lives but then put on a uniform and appear to be the most honorable, amazing people.

I think it's hard for an 18-year-old kid who doesn't really know who he is to be in a group with so many diverse people. There are plenty of negative influences in the Army. There are bad apples everywhere. But if you're smart, you seek out the positive influences. You sit down and you talk to them, and you take a little bit from each one to make yourself better. I was taking a little bit of everybody's approach, and maybe taking a little bit of everybody's personality, as I was finding my way.

When the year was up, we all had the option to stay in Korea or move on. Staying another year meant that I would be promoted and have the chance to influence young soldiers, just as VanValkenburg influenced me. I decided I would stay. Besides, I liked it in Korea. Lyle and Yacobucci stayed with me, and Nancy and I went on to participate in several marathons at different Army posts around Korea.

Alex Rosa left after a year. He went on to be assigned

to the 89th Military Police Brigade in Fort Hood, Texas. Later, he was stationed in Iraq, and in 2007, an improvised explosive device detonated near his vehicle in Muqdadiyah and killed him. He was 22. His wife Melissa, who also was in the military, became a widow after just eight months of marriage. Their daughter, Ellie, was only a month old, the same age Alex was when his father was murdered.

DUTY STATIONS

After my first year in Korea, I was promoted several times and assigned to the traffic accident investigation office. That's where I met Jennifer Berrios. It was only the two of us and a pair of Korean soldiers in the office.

Berrios was a hardscrabble Puerto Rican kid from Miami who spoke with a really thick accent. She hated wearing dresses. She'd cut off her T-shirt sleeves and wear them on her head. The one conservative thing about her was her faith. She and her whole family were very conservative Catholics.

I quickly saw that Jennifer was the most organized

and efficient person that I had encountered in the military, and that's saying something. All and all, she was simply one of the most squared-away people I had ever met. "You're the coolest dude I know," I'd always tell her.

"Shut the fuck up," she'd always respond. "I'm a *girl*."

Our job was to investigate any traffic accidents that happened in our area, on or off base, that involved an American citizen. We had our own patrol vehicle. We'd go out and liaise with the Korean police and write a report on the accident that had to be sent to the Army. The Army would then send it to the American embassy, and from there, it would go to all kinds of places.

Berrios and I were both E-4s at that point, but we had this immense responsibility that affected international relations. Both of us took it very seriously, maybe a little too seriously. Often the two of us would catch ourselves admonishing the Korean police because they had missed a step or had done something wrong.

Berrios and I became close because we worked together every day. We also had a similar interest in exploring Korea. Her ethos about Korea was: "We're only going to be here once. We're going to do absolutely everything and see absolutely everything."

I got a bicycle, and we would ride together for miles and miles all over Busan. Because she was from Miami, Jennifer wasn't scared of cycling through urban areas at all. I was the opposite. We would be in a major intersection with six lanes on each side and she'd tell me to move into traffic.

"Dude, seriously, we're going to get run over!" I'd complain.

"Whatever, just follow me. I got this!" And she'd just jump into the traffic, get right in there with the vehicles, and ignore the red lights.

She'd wake me up at 5 am on a damned Saturday with her bike helmet on and a little backpack, already in her adventure clothes. My Korean roommate would be cussing and crying, "Get out of here!"

Berrios always had intricate plans: "We're going to go on a bike ride, we're going to go to this mountain range over here, and we're going to hike up it."

"What the hell, Jen. It's five o'clock in the morning."

"I know. I've already been up for an hour."

During my last couple of months in Korea, I enrolled in the primary leadership development course. It's required for anyone who gets promoted to sergeant. I trained for about a month away from my actual unit on a little tiny base up in the northern part of Korea. So even before we all left, things were changing for my group of friends from Basic.

It's a universal truth that applies to everybody in the military: you meet so many awesome people that you only know for a short time, and then you never see them again.

Once you get orders from the Permanent Change of Station (PCS) to transfer out of Korea and go somewhere else, you start the process of clearing. It's on you to go through all the paperwork and start ticking items off the checklist that you need in order to go to your next duty station. In my case, it was off to Alaska. But not directly.

When I left Korea, I first flew into Dallas and picked up an F-150 that I had bought in Oklahoma during an earlier leave. After a couple of weeks with my family, I went to Georgia for Airborne School and then drove back to Dallas and shipped the truck to Alaska. Jump school lasted three weeks; it was a procedural type of a school and almost boring.

From Georgia, I went to Anchorage to join the rest

of the 4-25 Airborne. A familiar face greeted me at the airport: April Law, a battle buddy from Basic. She was working as an MP there, which I always thought was appropriate given her last name.

It's hard to leave good people behind, but the people who you've served with become like brothers and sisters. If you ever see them again, even after a long time, it's like you haven't missed a beat. It was like that when Law picked me up from the airport and drove me to the reception unit at Fort Richardson.

The base was not ready for the influx of people brought on by the new unit. They told me, "You're single, so you need to stay in the barracks room." I had heard that people were moving off post and abandoning the barracks rooms. I turned in my barracks key and got an apartment off base. It was right outside the Air Force base gate. The apartment was relatively cheap by Alaska standards, but there was a reason. It was in a terrible neighborhood. At times, my neighbors would ask me if I was a cop, and of course I'd say "no."

"Well, why the hell are you in this neighborhood?"

I told them the truth: "Because it's cheap."

Since we set up the 4-25 as a new unit, there just wasn't enough equipment there for us; it was still being delivered. We didn't have Humvees, jackets, or any-thing. A lot of people would stick around the office and say, "I can't work because I don't have equipment. They haven't given it to me yet."

Screw that, I thought. The Army had a mission for us to do in Iraq, and our commanders allowed us to start training without gear. I bought a Gore-Tex jacket and joined my platoon in training. We would drive our personal vehicles out to the different weapons ranges. (This is usually forbidden, for good reason.)

Alaska was like another planet. You know you're in a crazy Arctic environment when the first indicator that it's starting to warm up is when it *starts* snowing. It was literally too cold for it to snow. We attended classes that taught us what to do if we encountered a bear or moose. Every parking spot on post had a heater to keep engines warm enough to start.

Alaska was primarily a training ground for Iraq. We all knew this. We were mostly training for convoy secu-rity. Roadside bombs were a major threat to convoys, but we also learned how to keep convoys from being attacked directly and how to respond if we were hit.

The Army had virtual reality trainers housed inside big semi-truck box trailers. You would walk in and be surrounded by screens. It was like being in a live-action video game. They put you in all these scenarios, and you'd practice how you'd react. One of the trainers was for rollovers. It had an actual Humvee you'd sit in, and you'd learn how to get out while wearing all your gear.

Since I was the only single NCO, I volunteered for training missions. I would be assigned to oversee little elements on these trips. It was great to be in charge and get specialized training, but it was also an opportunity for me to finally see my country.

For example, I took 11 MPs down to Missouri to a course called Search and Destroy. It taught us how to locate explosives and respond to all different types of improvised explosive device (IED) scenarios. We scoured vehicles, houses, buildings, structures, and roads.

One of my buddies in the course had been stationed at Fort Leavenworth and was familiar with the area. "I think you guys have time for a little tour of St. Louis," he said. We loaded into a Chevrolet Suburban, and he drove us all around St. Louis. The most shocking parts, to me, were the high-crime neighborhoods of East St. Louis.

It was not something I would soon forget. The

streets were dark. Streetlights either didn't exist or had long been broken. Trash burned in the streets in barrels. It was an education to us all. At that point, the only foreign country I had been to was Korea. This trip really exposed me to the divide between different classes in my own country. I thought I'd have to leave the United States to see people living in those conditions.

Later, when I got to Iraq, I saw the same kind of neighborhoods in Baghdad and came to a really sad realization: "This looks just like East St. Louis."

JUMPING INTO THAILAND

I wasn't supposed to be the senior guy in charge of soldiers during a trip to Thailand, but it worked out that way. Staff Sergeant Coe had a family emergency and had to bow out, which is not something that the Army usually lets you do, but we had a great platoon sergeant in Mark Powell who really looked out for us. You usually go where you are told. I was the second in charge, and SFC Powell believed in me and made me step up.

I was 21 and in way over my head.

It was to be a weeklong joint training operation with Thai paratroopers. I was responsible for bringing 10 MPs and one medic to Thailand, keeping them out of trouble, and getting them back home again.

We boarded a C-17 in Anchorage and flew straight to Lopburi, Thailand. That's where we'd step out of the C-17 at an altitude of around 1,000 feet.

Our helmets were a concern when we were jumping into Thailand. Even if it's strapped on securely, the helmet could fall off your head. It was a terrible design, and thankfully, the military has gotten rid of it. If you lost your helmet, there was nowhere to get another one in Thailand, so they briefed us on the airplane to be careful during the jump.

When we jumped, the parachute of one of my soldiers must have caught on the edge of his helmet and pulled it right off of his head. I didn't know it until he told me on the ground. "Are you serious? After all that bullshit we had to go through," I said. "I told you a million times to secure your helmet!"

I had to go up to the sergeant major, a guy I didn't even know, and right off the bat tell him one of my guys had lost his helmet. We were attached to an infantry battalion, separated from our own organic chain of command, supposedly to keep the infantrymen in line while they were in Thailand. That already made us the bad guys that nobody wanted to talk to. Now, I was the bad guy in the chain of command's eyes, too.

We were starting off in Thailand on the wrong foot.

I didn't drink while I was in Thailand because I had to keep such a close eye on all my men, many of whom were acting foolish. They were 18- and 19-year-olds in Thailand. And what do you do in Thailand? You party because you're away from home there are no rules in Thailand.

Working with the Thai troops came first. They took us out to the jungle to visit different units. They have a thing about snakes. At one point, we sat in a circle and a guy came out with a burlap sack. When he opened it up, a king cobra stood up on its tail like a human being. It looked us in the eyes and the guy kept saying, "Whatever you do, do not run. If you run, it's going to chase you, and it's going to catch you. It's going to kill you."

I'm pretty good at following instructions, but I was worried about one of my guys who was terrified of snakes. I was worried he would panic and get killed on my watch. By a freaking snake.

Thai troopers are excellent at jungle warfare. We

learned all kinds of cool skills. Trees were tapped for fresh water, rice cooked inside bamboo stalks, snakes skinned and eaten. We would cook what we captured in the jungle, and that meant me eating freshly caught jungle rat.

I struggled to keep the guys in line because Thailand is one big frat party. I took a page out of my mom's book and told them, "I know you're going to drink, and I know you're underage. Let's all stay together. If you do this stuff in front of me, I won't stop it, but I will make sure you get back to your room at night and don't go to jail."

This led to some eye-opening field trips. On one of the last weekends in Thailand, we went to Bangkok.

One of the guys wanted to go to a nightclub there, and I didn't know what that meant exactly until I got there and witnessed two real human beings on stage having sex in a public show. The world was both bigger and more decadent than I had ever imagined.

Another night, we loaded into a taxi and asked the driver to take us to a good club. He pulled up to what looked like a hotel, and we all got out. Inside, we found a hallway lined with glass windows that opened to small showrooms. There were prostitutes inside each one, standing on couches and lounges in all these provocative positions. It was a menu, and they offered every different type of person you could imagine. Because of their age, a lot of the prostitutes in those rooms would be illegal anywhere else.

Some of the guys wanted to stay out of curiosity; I pulled them out right away. On the next taxi ride, they laughed about some of the things they saw inside. "Human trafficking," I said. "Yeah, it's fricking hilarious."

GET REAL, WE'RE IN IRAQ

In the fall of 2006, I was flying into Baghdad International Airport in an Air Force C-17 when the airplane plunged toward the earth.

When you think about how an airliner lands, you envision it descending gradually. Well, it doesn't *have* to. Aircraft were often being shot at from the ground, so the Air Force was doing very steep angled descents into Baghdad to minimize the risk. The faster you land the transport planes, the less time there is to take shots at them.

The Air Force pilots were flying at high altitudes, landing quickly, and then getting back off the ground. They warned us about this, but it was gut-wrenching, and people got sick in their seats. I thought we were falling out of the sky.

When we landed, we immediately knew we were in a combat zone. Before the doors even opened, I heard gunfire and explosions. We arrived at night, and when we left the aircraft, we saw orange patches on the horizon. It wasn't a natural phenomenon; there were fires burning in different parts of the city.

All right, time to get real, I thought. *We're in Iraq.*

We spent a couple of days in Baghdad before we boarded helicopters to the smaller areas where we were to be stationed. We did all of our flying at night, and the bases were all on black-out. You got used to walking in the dark.

We flew south of Baghdad to Forward Operating Base (FOB) Kalsu. Before we landed, they started deploying the flares; we were under fire as we were landing. At a certain time during the flight, they told us to lock and load. The Army is very safety conscious, so you know that when you are ordered to put a magazine into your weapon, it's got to be pretty serious.

As we landed, the FOB was under attack. If you're the enemy and you see aircraft coming in, that's a huge opportunity. As soon as we landed, the crew chief jumped out, pointed to the first person, and then pointed to where that person should run.

Our first couple of minutes at the FOB were spent in a bomb shelter, a type of concrete carport that they had all over Iraq. The whole time during this chaos, I was focused on trying to keep track of the soldiers who were with me.

A master sergeant handed out assignments for housing and a printed-out map. We headed off to our "cans," shipping containers that we would then modify. There were two beds, one on either end of the shipping container, with windows and a door carved into the walls. That's how we all lived.

More flights came in behind us, pretty much all night. Every time one would land, we'd receive more rockets and mortars, and we'd scurry back into the bomb shelter bunker. At some point during the night, we were ordered to gather in formation, which is highly frowned upon because big groups attract incoming fire. But we had to make sure everybody was accounted for.

The next day, we immediately went down to the

detainment facility to start working. The detainment facility is a place to house prisoners on a short-term basis. There was training to take care of first, since convoy training had been our pre-deployment focus. The Army needed us to conduct detainee operations, and so that's what we did.

Most of the time, we were with the prisoners. We would take them out to go to the bathroom, to the showers, or to exercise—that sort of prison guard work. We spent most of our time doing shifts at the detention facility or taking people to different appointments, such as medical visits and court dates. We'd move Iraqi nationals to different facilities around Iraq, which usually meant convoys. We took a helicopter only when transporting a high-value individual.

Once or twice a week, there would be a mission outside the wire that I would volunteer for. The married soldiers didn't volunteer for those, for good reason. At the time, though, I was a young, rambunctious twenty-something, and I wanted to go to combat.

In Iraq, we were overtaxed and undermanned. We worked 14-hour days with no days off. About seven months in, the Army extended our 12-month tour deployment to a 15-month tour. It was an emotional gut punch to the soldiers who were married with kids back home. And then we lost SFC Powell, when he was promoted. Sergeant Powell was a fine and intelligent man who really cared about his soldiers; he was always ready to listen and teach. When we lost him, morale tanked in the platoon.

Not for me, though. I liked being in Iraq because I liked not having to deal with real life and its petty controversies and silly dramas. I was in mission mode all the time. It would have suited me to stay over there for years. Your savings account just keeps growing because of combat pay and you're not spending your money because the Army takes care of everything you need.

Finally, after eight months, we got reinforcements from Fort Stewart in Georgia. They came in as part of the surge, and extra soldiers arrived to help us out. The work hours decreased but the danger increased. The Iran-backed militias were not happy about the surge, and they wanted to show us their response. They ramped up their rocket and mortar attacks on our bases. For hours on end, we were attacked.

I developed certain sensitivities in Iraq. I learned that rockets and mortars have certain sounds as they fly through the air. When I heard those whistling sounds getting louder, I knew that they were moving closer to me. We sustained a lot of losses in our battalion, but luckily, I didn't lose any of my friends. Still, it hurt.

One of the lessons I took from my time in Iraq is the awareness that there are some things in the world that the United States can't fix. I commend our country for going over there, but I found that good intentions and domestic political identity mean nothing to some people in the world. At the end of the day, some people are just going to hate you. It doesn't matter if I listen to NPR in the mornings or Sean Hannity in the afternoons, if I wear that uniform, they hate me. That's just because that's who they are and that's what they have been led to believe. As a young, idealistic soldier, this was a shock.

OBJECTIVE: COLLEGE

While I was in Iraq, I took college courses over the Internet. I would be sent a CD with all the lectures and videos, and then I would send back my papers and homework. I racked up a fair number of credits that way. But I knew that I still didn't have enough credits to become a commissioned officer. I would have to finish my four-year degree somewhere.

During the end of my deployment, with around six weeks left, I put in for the Reserve Officers' Training Corps (ROTC) Green to Gold Active Duty Option. It's the best-kept secret in the Army. You go to school for two years at a university of your choice, attend ROTC a couple of times a week, and get paid full active duty pay and benefits while you're doing it. For 21 months, at least.

When I got back from Iraq, during my well-earned leave, I began emailing different universities around Dallas. I wanted to go back home for a couple of years, so my first choice was University of Texas at Arlington. The university that gave me the most credits, however, was the University of North Texas (UNT) in Denton, so UNT it was. It was an exciting opportunity because the school was starting a brand-new ROTC battalion, and I'd be a big part of that.

I settled into an apartment in Denton for under $500 a month, all expenses included. It was recommended by the university, but it was a private apartment complex only for students. I filled out a personality profile, and they matched me with a roommate. It was a four-bedroom apartment, and I roomed with three education majors, two of whom were dating. It was a good situation because my roommates were pretty mature and there weren't a lot of parties.

They got me out and about more than I would have been on my own. I'm too pragmatic to use my time to be social. I'm not one to hang out with a crowd just to be with people. I need to realize tangible benefits from how I spend my time. I think the Army taught me that.

The ROTC program at UNT was a full-time job for me. There were four of us upperclassmen. I was the only one who had any real military experience. I was still making E-6 active duty pay and benefits.

One day while I was in the ROTC office, my friend Jennifer Berrios called me. I could tell she was beating around the bush trying to tell me something. "Hey, remember what you've always told me...um...you know...."

I knew where she was going with this, so I quickly replied, "Are you finally going to tell me you're a lesbian? Because I've known for, like, several years now. And yeah, I always told you I knew."

"So, you're okay with that?" she asked.

"Uh, so why not?" I said, relishing the moment. "I'm gay, so why would I *not* be okay with it?"

After she told me about being a lesbian, I felt like we were that much closer. "But how did you know I was a lesbian before I did?" she wanted to know.

"I don't know how you *didn't* know," I told her. "Everybody did. Everybody who is close to you, I mean. To us, it's pretty obvious. You're just the coolest dude I know."

"Shut up," she snapped back. "I'm a *girl*."

I always loved Berrios; she's such an awesome person. Not long after our conversation, she and her girlfriend were both deployed to Iraq and were both injured. Berrios was injured by shrapnel. After they returned from Iraq, they got married, went from Fort Hood back to the Fort Lauderdale area, and bought a house. They took advantage of the G.I. Bill and went to school. I knew I would be seeing them again.

My time as a student at UNT was a lot of fun. I met some really great people. One of the people I went to ROTC with, a woman I was really close with, became one of the first female Army Ranger school graduates in history. Our commanding officer there was Major

Hermann Troy, Jr. and he had extremely high expectations. I feel like he prepared us well to become officers.

TRAVIS

In June I had to report to Fort Benning, Georgia. I was reporting for the basic officer leadership course, but my class didn't start for another month. We had to wait for the people who were coming in from West Point to get there. That was already bad news. West Point people are idiots. It's like working with a bunch of privileged rich kids who never had any adversity in their lives. It's terrible.

During the wait, Jen Berrios and her wife Jaime texted one day and told me they wanted to visit. They came to my apartment in Columbus, and they wanted to go out for some nightlife in Atlanta. I realized later that they were worried about me because I was a gay guy in infantry training, and that can be the hardest part of the Army.

They wanted to go to a gay club in Atlanta. I hate going to gay clubs; they're the worst ever. But they pulled me along anyway. While we were there, a girl came up to me while I was standing in line at the bathroom and started flirting, saying that she "just loved my jawline."

I muttered something back like, "All right, well, nice to meet you." She was acting like an awkward weirdo, and she wasn't leaving. I was about to go in the bathroom when she blurted out, "Hey, why are you here? You know this is a gay bar, right?"

I told her it was pretty freaking obvious.

Finally, she asked if I was gay, and I said yes. "Why are all the good ones gay?" she sighed. She turned around and motioned for some dude who was standing at the bar to come over.

In the gay world, you have to be extremely careful. You can't just go up to a guy and hit on him. So, clearly, the guy standing over at the bar had sent in a girl first to make sure I was fair game.

The dude's name was Travis. I shook his hand, like I did with everybody else pre-pandemic. I don't ever hit on people; I just don't. It's not my thing. The only time I ever get involved with anybody is when they hit on me first.

I blew him off. I wasn't in a place in my life where I

wanted any kind of relationship. I was trying to focus on my career. Besides, we were only 90 minutes from post, close enough to make me uncomfortable in the era of "Don't ask, don't tell."

I went back over to Jaime and Jen, who were watching me the whole time. They wanted to know who the guy was. "I don't know," I said. "Some weirdo. He didn't have the balls to come talk to me himself, so he sent his girlfriend."

"Would you calm down? Can you relax for even five minutes?" Jaime asked. Berrios knew better and said, "He's not ever going to relax."

I became increasingly annoyed as the night went on. It got worse when the drag queens showed up. The way I see it, the more flamboyant gay people act, the more they make the rest of us look bad.

Travis found me at the bar. "I'm sorry about my friend earlier," he said. In my head, I was giving him credit for being persistent.

"That was kind of a cowardly move, to be honest with you," I said. "Why didn't you just come up and talk to me?"

As we talked, he seemed pretty cool. He'd played football in high school, and so he seemed like my kind of guy. At the end of the night, he said he wanted a sober ride home. I hadn't been drinking at all; I'd seen too many consequences working traffic investigations in Korea to ever drink and drive.

The four of us piled into my four-door Chevy Silverado. That's when he admitted that he was staying with somebody. This raised a red flag: he doesn't have his own place. By the time we got to the house, both women were on guard against him.

When we pulled up, Berrios asked to use the bathroom. I was ready to stay and chill out, but they were being really pushy, and we left. She later told us that she had searched through the bathroom and found some pills in the cabinet that she didn't think were prescription. When we got back into the truck, she said I shouldn't ever talk to him again.

Several days went by, and I was taking their advice. The week was horrible, though, stuck out in the field with a bunch of rambunctious idiots from West Point. They thought it was funny to act gay. They were out there singing Ricky Martin songs, dry humping each other, and being ridiculous.

During that time, the "Don't ask, don't tell" policy was being debated by Obama's people. It was a huge deal where I was at Fort Benning. Everybody was always talking about it because the president was talking about it. And it wasn't helpful dialogue. I heard many different slurs.

The cavorting West Pointers really irked me. The people I was training with all had bachelor's degrees. They were all educated, but they were all extremely bigoted as a group. Nobody knew about my personal life. However, I was the only prior enlisted guy, so they kind of looked up to me. At the worst of their antics, I would just shake my head and silently say, *You guys are a bunch of idiots.*

I've found that it's extremely rare for one person to have the fortitude to stand up and say, "You guys are all wrong and I'm not going to follow this line of conversation." It's unusual to find somebody like that, especially somebody who's straight. It'd be easy for me to do that because I'm just defending myself. They didn't know I was gay at that point, but still it'd be easier for me to do that. To me, it means more if it comes from somebody who's not gay. It's the same as if somebody says something racist around me. If I allow that to go unchallenged, then I'm a coward, right?

I was really fed up dealing with all their nonsense throughout the week. So, on Friday, I said to myself,

I'm going to drink. I was drinking at my apartment when Travis texted me: "Hey can I call you?" We talked on the phone a little while and I decided that I was going to give this guy a chance.

I was attracted by his looks, but I also thought he was cool. I came to find out that he had had his driver's license revoked because he had a DUI. That was a massive turnoff. I've investigated way too many DUIs, and I know what you can do to innocent people when you drink and drive. I found out he was driving on an expired license and he still didn't have a place of his own.

I started thinking that Travis was trouble. I went several weeks without communicating with him, but he was persistent, and I finally responded. I talked to him because there was nobody else to talk to in rural Georgia. And he was a very attractive guy; he just didn't have his life together. Maybe I could help.

I told him I'd make a deal. I would hang out with him if he started his community service. That was the first step to get his driver's license back. "I don't want to do that," he said.

"You're like six foot four, 240 pounds," I said. "Why are you whining like such a little baby?"

It worked, at least for a little while. His mom even reached out to me and told me that she was so happy that Travis was getting back on track. His parents invited me over to a fish fry and I saw they were my kind of people.

I decided I was going to give Travis another chance. As the months rolled past, I made him do stuff. I would tell him, "I'm not coming back up there and staying in somebody else's house." He finally got his license back and got an apartment.

Travis was pressuring me hard to get out of the Army. I listened to him and friends like Jen Berrios. Everyone was saying I should leave. I wasn't feeling the whole officer thing at Fort Benning anyway. I saw almost immediately when I got there that the officer world was very different from the enlisted world. In the officer world, you're all alone.

To use a sports metaphor, you're a free agent when you're an officer, but when you're enlisted, you're always part of a team. It's good for some people, not good for others. I didn't want to fight the war by myself; I wanted to be part of a team.

It seemed like my Army career was coming to an end. I went to a lawyer to get out of the Army under

"Don't ask don't tell." I paid the lawyer $700, and he wrote me a one-page memorandum.

I took the memorandum to my commanding officer, Colonel Scott Halstead. He read it and asked with concern, "Why did you think you had to go to a lawyer?"

He got on the phone and called my company commander and the commander of the headquarters company. He gave them strict guidance on what to do. Then he called me back in and warned me about my classmates, saying that it may not be a good idea to tell them, as they were not yet mature enough to handle it. I agreed and thanked him for being so professional.

Days later, I was moved to the headquarters company while I was doing my out-processing. When I got there, I was assigned as an assistant to the executive officer for the battalion. The executive officer of the battalion, Major Andrew Sinden, had a lot of different projects going on because a new headquarters complex was being built. He was overwhelmed with work and needed an assistant. I spent a lot of time wearing a hard hat, doing inspections with the Corps of Engineers, and looking at blueprints. It was a really interesting job, and it stretched on for months.

I made post-Army plans. I interviewed with the

Atlanta and Columbus police departments. I went to the Columbus PD for a PT test and all the background checks. They even logged into my Facebook page and snooped around.

That's when Travis, the one who had convinced me to get out of the Army, broke up with me. I guess he got tired of me bossing him around in ways that I thought would set him on a more productive path. After six months, he texted me and just said, "This is not going to work."

NEXT STOP, AFGHANISTAN

I was working with Major Sinden and plotting to leave the Army when Obama made the decision to get rid of "Don't ask, don't tell."

Colonel Halstead called me into his office. "Look, to be honest with you, we have not gotten any guidance for some time," he said, referring to my request to leave military service. "The commanding general has your request, and he's been reluctant to send it to the secretary of the Army because we've all been expecting the president to do this. I believe that, even if the commanding general sends it to the secretary of the Army, that it will be sent back to him and without action because of this presidential order."

"So, what do you want to do?" he continued. "You can wait for several months, and wait on the likely denial, or we can go ahead and just tell the general right now to tear it up."

"All right, let's just tear it up. I'll just go back to work."

So just like that, I went back into training and finished out the basic officer leader's course. Luckily, the class that I went into was not stocked with terrible West Point graduates. I was with my kind of people, the ROTC and Officer Candidate School (OCS) people, and had a good time with the rest of the basic officer leader's course.

Ranger school came next, but I suffered a heat injury that made me ineligible to go back until the winter. I couldn't just hang around Fort Benning doing nothing, so they sent me to Fort Bragg, and from there, I almost immediately went to Fort Irwin, California, for a monthlong immersive training at the National Training Center.

The other officers and I had known even before we

got to Fort Bragg that we were going to Afghanistan. We were in the life cycle of a brigade combat team, which was three years. All of us got to Fort Bragg at around the same time, and we would be deploying around the same time.

We also knew that we were going to Regional Command South. As the time of deployment grew closer, we learned that we were going to Kandahar, so we tailored our reading material to that location. We even knew where our battalions and companies were going to be stationed. This is something that struck me as being very different from when I was an enlisted soldier. As an enlisted soldier, I was expected to know my job really well. As an officer, though, you're a big-picture guy who is supposed to know everything that's going on. They want you to become an expert about where you're going, to learn as much as you can before you get there.

To do that, you've got to do your homework. As soon as my battalion received pinpoint orders, the senior officers in the battalion started to do officer professional development sessions. There were books to read and essays to write on top of training our troops to shoot, move, and communicate.

It was important to me to try to understand the

different psychology and personality of the average Afghan. They are extremely different from average Americans. In America, we feel comfortable knowing that the rule of law exists. If someone's done something wrong, there are ways to fix it that don't involve blowing up their car, shooting an AK-47, or planting an IED in their driveway.

One of the things I learned about Afghanistan before I went over was that there's corruption everywhere. Transparency International's Corruption Perceptions Index routinely ranks the nation among the top five of most corrupt countries. Everybody is involved in it. We were going to have to be judicious in how we dealt with people because we wouldn't know their true intent. Everybody there knows that the Afghan government is trying to play two sides of the coin. On one side is the United States, and on the other are the drug lords who are really controlling the security of the country.

The Army, especially at Fort Bragg, did a good job of helping us learn about the enemy. There were a lot of materials coming out of Afghanistan in real time. The unit that was there ahead of us, the one we were going to replace, was sending us reports on a daily or hourly basis. We devoured those reports. We were all trying to build a mental picture of what the operation looked like in Afghanistan, especially what the enemy was doing. As an infantry officer, the vital question for me to ask was: "What is the enemy likely to do next?"

We knew that the tactic at that time was for the Taliban to use motorcycles and dirt bikes to attack us and get away quickly. They'd ride out of these big, dry canals known as *wadis*, take shots or throw grenades, and then dart back into the canals to escape. They would disappear back into the earth.

There was no way for us to chase them. We were like cyborgs over there with all of our protective equipment and gear. We were not mobile at all. I heard we had funds approved to buy motorcycles for ourselves. The plan was to put one or two American paratroopers on a motorcycle and launch them in pursuit of an Afghan who'd attacked us on motorcycle. We were basically trying to figure out how to catch them, or at least keep them at a distance.

The threat posed by motorcycles was made very clear to me long before we deployed. What I didn't know was that a platoon under my direct command would be facing them on the battlefield.

PART II

AFGHANISTAN

February 2012

WHEN WE WENT INTO COMBAT, the entire brigade went with us. To get 3,500 people to Afghanistan, the Army would first charter civilian airliners to get us close to the border. It's like you're on a commercial flight except everybody is in the same uniform and there are machine guns at your feet.

We landed in Manas, Kyrgyzstan, in February. Manas is a relatively safe city in Afghanistan's neighboring country Kyrgyzstan. Our chartered flights landed at Manas's international airport in February. In a quiet corner of the giant international airport, there's a tiny US Air Force base. As soon as we landed, the military buses arrived to take us there. Inside the small base, there were Quonset huts lined up in rows and tents everywhere. It was basically a tent city, but with a gym and everything you might find in a big hotel.

Getting into Afghanistan was more complicated because it was a combat zone and subject to a variety of flight restrictions. That created a bottleneck at Manas, which had become a staging area for those going into Afghanistan. We spent about two weeks in Manas being processed. I spent a lot of time at the coffee shop there, looking at real estate and truck listings at the Internet café.

There are two types of soldiers in the Army: the combat soldier and the support soldier. The support soldiers never leave the bases, and, of course, they were happy as larks. They weren't taking the war as seriously as they should have, but those of us who knew we were going to be in combat felt differently.

A large majority of guys in the Army are 18 years old and just want to go to war. However, the mood of everybody who knew what was coming was very somber. Officers heard briefings about the conditions in Afghanistan in the Arghandab valley, the birthplace of the Taliban. We knew there was going to be some rough fighting; we could see that just from reading the casualty reports from the units that were already there.

The mood darkened even more when word came back about a casualty among our advance troops. I'm not sure exactly what base he was on, but one of our first sergeants was shot in the back of the head by an Afghan National Security Forces troop, supposedly an ally. Before we even had all our boots on the ground, we were losing paratroopers to insider attacks.

Finally, the same bus that took us to the base arrived to ferry us to a C-17, which I consider the Cadillac of Air Force aircraft. There's plenty of space in them. There were at least five of them on the tarmac that morning, enough to accommodate the hundreds of Army troops heading into combat. Against a backdrop of old buildings that hadn't been updated in decades, beautiful brand-new C-17s were lined up and looking absolutely gorgeous.

I get motivated by little things like that.

Our C-17 landed at the massive airbase at Kandahar. It's a NATO base, so every one of our allied military forces is represented at this base, and that's why it's so big. They include units from Japan and some smaller countries such as Montenegro that don't want to or can't get involved in combat operations. These tenant units live full time at the base, but they never go out on patrol.

Kandahar is a giant city, and I was not expecting that. It has paved roads, traffic lights, fire stations, a big hospital—everything. It's not a beautiful city; it's actually disgusting, ugly, and beaten down. The buildings are all shot up, and you can tell they've been blown up several times. Many of them were crumbling, and American engineers had come in and put in structural reinforcements. This big city was trying to thrive, against all odds, and the Taliban wasn't having any of it.

Walking around and seeing all of these structures that really shouldn't be standing, but somehow still were, was oddly inspirational. They were examples of resilience, something we would all need to survive the battlefield.

We arrived at Forward Operating Base (FOB) Pasab by helicopter. The base was located near Zhari, on the north bank of the Arghandab River. Most buildings are single-story mud structures except for the tall grape-drying huts.

I was a squadron liaison officer in the tactical operations center (TOC) at the FOB. A TOC is the coordination center for all the different war-fighting assets in any given area. Afghanistan is chopped up into precincts, and every brigade has its own area of operations.

The TOC had a giant room with stadium-style seating, with long desks, chairs at computer stations, radios, and so on. It was staffed with soldiers and airmen, Marines and sailors. The Afghan army and police were represented. Basically, everybody who had a stake in the fight had a representative in the TOC.

A big screen dominated one wall, flanked by a few smaller flat screens. All of these different screens displayed something happening on the battlefield. There were cameras everywhere in Afghanistan. Some of them were feeds from unmanned aerial vehicles, others were feeds from big blimps that we had tethered over bases, but all of them were in real time. These feeds kept you involved in what was taking place on the ground.

Everybody faced the front of the room, so the TOC sort of resembled a movie theater made of plywood. Almost everything on Army bases in Afghanistan is made out of plywood, except for the offices of the generals and admirals. In the military, there is no need to make anything look nice. It's just about getting things done in the most efficient and cheapest way.

Anytime there was a patrol outside the wire or any kind of a combat operation (any mission other than a logistical mission, such as a supply convoy), we tracked it at the battalion and brigade levels. This was both good and bad. When you're a leader on the ground, you are the one who has to make all the decisions, but you always have people watching you and second-guessing every decision you make.

They can interrupt a mission by trying to be helpful, calling and asking if the soldiers in the field need anything. You just want to beg them to chill out and let those in the field do their jobs. But there are plenty of people who have never been platoon leaders in Afghanistan or Iraq. They may have been platoon leaders in Kosovo or Desert Storm, but by the time they made colonel or general, they had no experience in actual combat leadership in Iraq or Afghanistan. When the situation is so fluid and complex, as it was with an insurgency raging outside the wire, it's better to provide the combat leaders with the tools they might need ahead of time and leave them to operate. One of my biggest jobs in Afghanistan was to try to anticipate what the troops might need next and have it ready for them just in case.

At the TOC, your job changes when the unit in the field reports Troops in Contact. Then it becomes a matter of responding. The commanders, like the colonels, can worry about the overall mission. Your mission is to make sure that the American and allied troops who are out there fighting have everything they need. When someone is injured, for example, you are among those in the TOC who must make sure that the medical helicopter gets dispatched from Kandahar airfield to the exact spot where it is needed.

For instance, when I had a patrol in my area that went outside the wire, I would watch on camera and listen to their radio calls. If they started reporting any kind of Troops in Contact, then I would turn to my left and right and ask, "Hey, what helicopter assets do you have right now? What assets do you have right now?" When my battalion asked for helicopter support, my job was to convince the battle captain to send them.

A normal workday for me was 20 hours long. That's just the way it is in combat. The enemy operates around the clock, so you've got to keep up. In combat, you never have time to think about anything. I think that's why some people have such a hard time when they get back. For the first time since the fighting started, they have a chance to think about what happened. There's no chance to do any kind of introspection or any kind of therapy while you're in the thick of combat.

As we settled into work, something else about Afghanistan became very clear. We knew that our own generals didn't support us. Our support stopped at the lieutenant colonel level. Anybody above that rank was a politician and did not have our best interests in mind. The best example of that was Colonel Brian Mennes. He would routinely blame his own paratroopers, in open forum, when they were injured by improvised explosives.

Mennes was a full-bird colonel who wanted everyone to know there was one stud at the helm, and that was him. Nobody else mattered. The only thing that mattered was his career and his promotion to general. He didn't develop his junior officers, which is always dangerous, but left them dependent on him to make decisions. The only thing that he cared about was getting his own promotion.

It was almost like an internship, working right there

with Colonel Mennes. As much as I despise the guy, he is a brilliant tactician. I think he doesn't have any morals. But he knows his tactics, and I learned a lot from him.

Colonel Mennes's command climate was more aggressive than that of any other brigade commander in the area, and that includes the Marines. I appreciated that environment because the Taliban was going to be aggressive, so we needed to be even more aggressive.

ROTC and OCS officers hated Mennes because we were blue-collar-type officers. There's definitely a divide in the officer corps in the Army along those lines. The blue-collar officers did not respect Mennes because we saw him for what he was: just another bully.

Still, he had plenty of support from people who wanted to be on his bandwagon. Anytime Colonel Mennes made a decision, people jumped on the bandwagon to show that they were on board with him. They did this so that their careers and paychecks would rise with his. And the sad thing is, it worked. Mennes is a general now, and he'll probably become a four-star general because he knows how to kiss butt.

In the TOC, I discovered there were significant

resources that were not being used. Division leaders would say, you've got this many helicopters for this 24-hour period, you've got these Navy jets, you've got this Air Force surveillance plane and whatever else was available. We would have what we call Operations Sync meetings where all the representatives from our battalions requested assets. It was incredible to me that nobody from my battalion was telling me, "We need helicopters from this time to this time tomorrow." Or "We need artillery support from this time." We had all these awesome assets but nobody was using them.

It remains unfathomable to me that an infantry officer would plan a mission and not ask for this kind of support. The enlisted men and women in the field who were getting their arms and legs blown off could have really used a helicopter above them to help them defeat the Taliban. But their officers were not asking for that sort of badly needed support.

Here I was as a first lieutenant making the decision for a lieutenant colonel to ask the Army to give us helicopters to support our troops. I was a first lieutenant, and making those decisions was way above my pay grade, but all the lieutenants were doing it. The disconnect between the frontline soldiers and their commanders was appalling.

All the lieutenants sat around and lamented, "Why the hell are these colonels not asking for this stuff? If it's available, why aren't they asking for it?" As junior officers, we were not expected or supposed to make those kinds of decisions. But in our case, if those critical decisions were going to be made, we had to make them.

Sometimes, I would sit down and have lunch with the helicopter pilots. They'd complain that nobody was using them. They told me that if nobody asks them to do anything, they just fly around in circles. The result of this created a reactionary type of environment. Only when a patrol would get attacked by the enemy would everyone's hair suddenly catch on fire. Often the patrols that suddenly and badly needed the support wouldn't get it because it had been allocated elsewhere.

If the infantry officers had done their homework and understood their environment a little better, they would have planned one step ahead. If I am planning on going into a village that has attacked us every time we've gone into it, maybe I should arrange for some helicopters ahead of time.

I got the schedule of the birds and all the other assets before I came into the regular meeting on asset assignments. The unmanned aerial vehicle (UAV) manager, a brilliant female sergeant first class, would announce, "Okay, we have UAVs [colloquially known as drones] from this time to this time. We've got a Predator from this time to this time." I was always the first guy to claim the assets. Since I was the only prior enlisted officer there, everybody kind of stepped back and let me have first choice. After several weeks, the UAV manager would start off the meetings with "Lieutenant Lorance, what do you want?" She knew I was going to ask for it anyway.

I started personally coordinating to make sure that military working dog teams would get on helicopters to go to specific locations for our operations. It was a rare instance where somebody would use a dog team, and it was always on a huge operation when a general was watching or something. Anytime that happened, the officers wanted to add these fancy assets.

The way I looked at it, there should have been dog teams on every operation because they were available. There should've been one on even mundane patrols because those kinds of missions are the ones where paratroopers lose legs. They shouldn't be reserved just for big sexy operations where generals are watching on big screens.

The dog kennels were tucked off in a corner of the base where I was stationed. They had their own little compound off the beaten path; you would never just happen to wander onto it because it was a closed compound. I started going over there and hanging out. There were about a dozen military working dog teams that weren't being used to their potential.

I developed a really good professional relationship with those in charge of the dog teams, to a point where they would email me: "Hey, L-T. I have a team that's available to go out next week from this time to this time." I would immediately get back to them and dispatch them somewhere without even asking anybody. I would call the unit a couple of days before and tell them, "Sir, you're getting a dog. Just so you know."

Because of the unorthodox way I did things as a liaison officer, the sergeant major put me in for a Bronze Star. I have a copy of the paperwork that he wrote up, and it still makes me happy to see that somebody actually noticed.

We were there to do a job, and nothing damages

motivation more than when soldiers know that their commanders do not care about them. It takes so much away from them. And we knew that the rot came from the top—from Washington, D.C.

"ONCE UPON A TIME, AFGHANS AND AMERICANS WERE FIGHTING..."

May 2, 2012

Story by Petty Officer 1st Class Farrukh Daniel, 1st Stryker Brigade Combat Team, 25th Infantry Division Public Affairs

ARGHANDAB DISTRICT, Afghanistan—Less than a year ago, the Arghandab valley was the most dangerous place in Afghanistan. The Soviets used to call the Arghandab River Valley "The Heart of Darkness." It's where Mullah Omar first formed the Taliban in 1994 and it's where the famous Battle of Arghandab was fought in 2008. Today, despite some long-suffering Taliban holdouts, the valley is a peaceful place. At least it is in the village of Kvah-jeh Molk. This is due in large part to the partnering and mentoring efforts of the brave warriors of Company A, 1st Battalion, 67th Armor Regiment.

Through partnering with the local Afghan Uniformed Police force and the Afghan local police, the village and the surrounding countryside serve as a model for what can be achieved when Afghanistan's National Security Forces take the lead throughout the country. In Kvahjeh Molk, a small community on the banks of the mighty Arghandab River, the bustling bazaar and scores of children running the streets are the image of what a peaceful Afghanistan can look like.... Once upon a time, Afghans and Americans were fighting and dying together in Arghandab district. Those days are gone. As the 2014 deadline for U.S. troop withdrawal inches closer, many people fear that once coalition forces leave, the Taliban will sweep back into power overnight on the backs of Afghan forces unable to stem the tide. To know whether the Afghans will be able to keep the peace, one need look no further than this tiny little village overlooking Afghanistan's most famous river.

"They're good," said Bartholomew. "They do it all without us. I'm sure when we leave, they'll keep doing it just the same."[*]

This is the kind of ridiculous misinformation the Pentagon was telling the American people about the Arghandab valley in 2012.

Washington, D.C., may have been telling people the war was winding down, but that was not the reality of the soldiers stationed in Afghanistan. Our forces were under fire on patrols, hounded by explosive devices, plagued by landmines, and ambushed by gunmen. The Taliban ran everything outside the base and had plenty of informants inside the wire.

We were supposed to think we were okay when we were on base, but we really weren't because of the insider threat. We couldn't even eat without bringing our loaded weapons to the chow hall.

Arghandab's got a bad reputation, even by Afghan standards. During the Soviet invasion, the people of the river valley repelled a Soviet onslaught. The Taliban's seat of government and Mullah Omar's house

---

[*] https://www.dvidshub.net/news/printable/87737

lay just across the region's southern boundary. It's one place Osama Bin Laden called home during his stay in Afghanistan.

Not surprisingly, the reality of the region is one of continuing violence and insurgency. As an example, take one week in June 2012 when I was there: three gunmen in Afghan police uniforms opened fire on U.S. troops, killing one and wounding three. Later that week in the Arghandab valley, eight insurgents made their way into the perimeter at Forward Operating Base Frontenac. Officials, according to CNN, "could not explain how the breach occurred, but initial reports indicate officials believe the insurgents might have had help from Afghan security personnel."[*] And that's just one week's worth of *reported* bad news. If this was what the Pentagon saw as "the image of what a peaceful Afghanistan can look like," those crafting the war's strategy were delusional.

If I really wanted to know what was going on in Afghanistan, I would ask a noncommissioned officer, one of the people actually doing the fighting. I would not ask a general or a colonel because they're going to give you the politically palatable answer. That's why,

---

[*] Barbara Starr, "Afghan Insurgents Strike U.S. Outpost," CNN, June 19, 2012.

despite the fact that we were losing ground, the number of units positioned in the Arghandab area was cut in nearly half from the height of the surge in October 2010.

The lies about progress in Afghanistan were all related to domestic politics in the United States, directed by the White House. We all felt the sting of the policies of the Obama administration on the frontline.

The rot went to the top. There's a great book by former Secretary of Defense Bob Gates in which he describes exactly how the Obama administration micromanaged the war. Gates said that he was concerned and frustrated as secretary of defense when the national security staff at the White House would bypass the Pentagon and give orders directly to U.S. forces. He felt it didn't make sense to even have a secretary of defense if the president was going to make all the decisions himself.

No White House dictate was more galling than the demands included in the rules of engagement (ROE), the set of conditions issued to combat troops under which the enemy can be engaged and killed. I would *never* say that the United States shouldn't be governed by any rules when going into war. We have to abide by the Geneva Conventions for many reasons, least of which because Americans fought and died to get them into place. But what the Obama administration demanded went far and above Geneva requirements.

For example, we could not shoot enemies if we ever lost a direct line of sight with them. If an enemy on a motorcycle plunges into a dry canal and pops up close by, he cannot be killed because no one had eyes on him the entire time. The line-of-sight restriction sapped morale because it meant that the assessment and the decisions of the commander on the ground did not matter, which is the exact opposite of what officers are meticulously trained to believe.

The choreographed way we were fighting also showed our enemy exactly what our weaknesses were, and they took advantage of them all the time. Our job as officers was to adapt to the enemy and defeat them on the battlefield, but the ROE would not let us do that.

Things were about to get worse. *The New York Times*[*] broke the news that a rogue U.S. Army sergeant "methodically killed" 16 civilians, nine of them children, in a rural district outside of Kandahar. Suffering from psychological wounds compounded by multiple back-to-back combat

---

[*] Taimoor Shah and Graham Bowley, "U.S. Sergeant Is Said to Kill 16 Civilians in Afghanistan," *The New York Times*, March 11, 2012.

deployments, the soldier had stalked house to house, shooting everyone he encountered. Rioting Afghans mobbed the Panjwai outpost. Afghan President Hamid Karzai called the killings "inhuman" and "unforgivable."

The Obama administration was quick to decry the attacks. Washington, D.C., needed to show that it could crack down on U.S. troops to appease the Karzai government. The welfare of the U.S. soldiers acting lawfully on the frontlines was the last thing considered in the calculus. The priority was an urgent diplomatic need to demonstrate that the U.S. Army could hold itself accountable—not how the soldiers on the frontlines might be affected.

That was our situation in Afghanistan under the Obama administration. They were trying to micromanage the war from Washington, D.C.—and it was getting soldiers killed.

THE HAND ON THE SHOULDER

I was sitting in the TOC, monitoring a Troops in Contact situation. I knew from the convoy reports that my battalion commander had arrived on the base, and normally, I would have gone to meet him. But I was too busy that day and didn't even see him until he came up behind me and put his hand on my shoulder.

I stood up, saying, "Sir, how are you doing?" He looked down at my feet. "I think you need to get some new boots. I'll have the S4 get you some." He was talking about the logistics officer, and I'll be damned if he didn't follow through. A couple of days later, the logistics captain brought me some brand-new boots.

"What's up, sir?" I asked, after thanking him for his concern over my boots.

"I just want to let you know that the sergeant major and I think you've done such a great job. I think that you've earned a platoon leader position. You're going to go down and take Lieutenant Latino's spot in Chainsaw."

Lt. Dominic Latino had been injured in combat, one of a string of casualties in the platoon, and his troops had been taken from their stronghold, Payenzai, for a mental health assessment. When they returned, they would need a lieutenant.

"When am I leaving, sir?" He told me I had two or three weeks. "Give me time to get somebody up here to replace you. You get them trained up and then we'll send you out."

"Roger that."

The guy who came in to replace me, Lieutenant Jared Leute, was a West Point guy. He defied the stereotype I had of those types. Happily, he started learning very quickly and I felt good about handing things to him. Nobody wants to just say, "Here you go" and then see everything that they've worked on go down the tubes. The stakes are too high for that.

Leute was coming from being a frontline platoon leader. It was a good opportunity for me. I was able to pick his brain about the do's and don'ts. I also heard his frustrations at the kind of waste of material he saw and the additional risk his men had taken in the field.

Once he got his footing, I transitioned almost a hundred percent to working out in the gym and preparing for my new assignment. I'd stop by intermittently to check on Leute, but I really didn't need to because he was so proficient.

The weeks before I went to Payenzai were all about homework. I wanted to know everything about the area I would be responsible for. I looked at the satellite imagery to scope out the area, including the natural features, population centers, and boundaries. Then I contacted my friend Lt. Katrina Lucas, an intelligence officer. I told her where I had been assigned and asked her if she could help me do some homework on my area.

She was more than happy to assist. She provided me a binder containing a variety of vital information. It identified high-value targets, with pictures and biometric details about the bad guys who were in our area. It also contained the specific objectives in the area and how they fit into the bigger picture. I spent a couple of weeks going over that material in great detail. She also gave me access to her workstation because I had security clearance. There, I was able to get a better picture of what was going on in Payenzai.

After working with Colonel Mennes and doing all this research, I knew what we were supposed to be doing there. The men of first platoon thought they had a special insight that came from being in the strong point for a few months, and in some tactical ways, they did. But when it came to the big picture, I had a firm grasp on my assignment.

I studied intelligence reports as if my life depended on it because it did. At the same time, I went around trying to find assets to take with me into the field that I could use to save lives. That's when I found a collection of coffin-sized storage containers with various parts to different drones or UAVs in them. The headquarters company commander was doing inventory when I went up to him and asked, "Sir, what are you going to do with all these UAV parts?"

"Well, they're just going to sit here 'cause nobody needs them."

"Well, can I have them?"

"Hell yeah, if you'll sign for them."

I didn't know for sure whether I was taking a functional UAV, but I knew that the boxes held a bunch of different parts. I just hoped that my soldiers would be able to piece them together.

I also leveraged the relationship that I had developed with the Air Force military working dog teams. Before I left to be a platoon leader, I told the handlers, "Make sure you always give me a dog. I'll always put it to use."

I saw that the company had just gotten a new camera tower. The old one was still operational, but it was just set off to the side. I asked the company commander what the plans were for the old camera tower, and he said, "Well, it's just going to sit there." So I asked, "Well, can I take it with me?"

"Well, yeah, if you'll sign for it."

The final step I wanted to take was to make sure there was a helicopter overhead when we went on patrol. I recalled my conversations with pilots who told me how frustrating it was to just loiter over the battlefield, doing racetrack patterns with nobody on the ground using them. So I told my successor at the TOC, Jared, "That'll never be an issue with me. Send me helicopters if you've got them and I'll use them."

I came in with a dog team, a camera tower, and a UAV—all resources the platoon had never before seen. I would never have known about all these resources had I not been working up in the TOC because you just don't see them as an infantry platoon leader. Their existence is outside your circle of understanding and you're never exposed to them.

I went above and beyond the scope of my duties to arrange for this gear. All the Army required of me was to show up and be the platoon leader, but I went the extra mile to help the soldiers on the ground.

TO PAYENZAI

I took a convoy from battalion headquarters to the company headquarters at Ghariban. I reported to the company commander and introduced myself.

We talked for a few minutes. That's when he told me that the platoon that I was taking over had some discipline problems. "I'm glad you're here. You need to go in hot and heavy and remind them that they are soldiers. They're forgetting who they are," he said.

He was very concerned about the platoon. He had seen them on convoys sporting beards and out of uniform. Another thing that concerned him was an incident that occurred during a combat patrol. One of the soldiers was shot, but they did not have the first aid bag there because they had forgotten it. Obviously, discipline in the platoon was lacking.

There was no ambiguity over what I was supposed to do. It was kind of like running onto the field at game time. I knew that it was time to play the game. I knew that it was time to do the job that I had been trained to do for years. But as soon as I stepped foot on the ground, I knew I would become the guy who would have to write a letter to a soldier's family if I screwed up.

I knew I could get the job done, period. But what I was most nervous and concerned about was my soldiers dying. I knew from working in the TOC that infantrymen died every day. I knew a very charismatic staff sergeant named Travis Mills. Everybody loved the guy. He lost both arms and both legs to a land mine. That was fresh in my mind. I knew that I was going into a dangerous area and I just didn't know how I would react if one of my soldiers were to step on an IED. Nobody knows how they're going to react to that situation.

When I took over, we had six weeks left in country, in combat. I was under no illusions that I would come in and try to win the war. Nobody's ever going to win that war. I was going to be the guy who either brought all the soldiers home or lost some at the end of the deployment.

All I thought about was how the hell to keep the enemy from killing my guys before we departed from a war that nobody gave a shit about anymore.

DAY ONE IN THE DORITO

After two days at company command, I went out to my platoon headquarters at Strong Point Payenzai. I called it a Dorito. It's shaped like a triangle, and there were guard towers on all three points of the triangle. Two tents had been set up there before I arrived, and the Afghan army was living in a small tent on the other side of the landing zone from where we slept.

The patrol base was one of the smallest I've ever seen. It was just big enough to land a Black Hawk helicopter in the middle. You want to make sure that if American or NATO helicopters experience some sort of trouble, they have somewhere friendly to set down. We couldn't land two of them at Payenzai at the same time, though. There wasn't enough room.

I brought a lot of equipment with me that the platoon had never seen before. I brought a pole with a camera, a UAV, and a dedicated dog team. All this stuff cluttered up the place a little bit, but it made us more effective.

From the reports I had been getting, I expected the

platoon to be an unorganized, ragtag group of soldiers. When I arrived, I saw more evidence of this. Their command post radio was lying on the floor between a couple of cots, right across from a PlayStation console. Sensitive items were strewn about, unsecure. I thought to myself, *My God. These people do not even identify as a military unit. They are a bunch of people out here camping.*

My first day with the platoon was also the platoon's first day back at the strong point after their psychological evaluation. They had been at the strong point for a couple of months before the break. They had been in combat for about four months before they got to Payenzai and they hadn't lost anybody. They didn't start losing people until they got to the strong point, but as soon as they did, they had four casualties. They were in the thick of things. The Taliban wanted very badly to take the position that we held.

When I arrived in Payenzai, first platoon soldiers told me that our company commander, Captain Patrick Swanson, never came down there because the area was too hostile.

I learned that the former platoon leader, Dominic Latino, was a "bro." He had "little man syndrome" and went above and beyond so everybody would think he was a cool guy. He was one of those people who's always trying to say clever things. He is probably popular on Instagram or TikTok.

Latino wanted his platoon to like him. I wanted his platoon to stay alive. That's all that I cared about. I could give a shit if they liked me or not. They were going to be alive at the end of the deployment. That was the difference in our two leadership styles.

Lieutenant Latino was medically evacuated after receiving shrapnel to his eyes, face, and abdomen from a Taliban attack. After he was injured, his troops were very upset. He was one of their good friends, one of the good ol' boys. Losing him really took away their will to fight.

I knew the platoon had issues. I knew that I could not go in there and just let them continue doing what that they had been doing. I knew that at some point in my tenure, I was going to have to piss off some people, both my subordinates and my superiors.

When I arrived at the strong point, I saw people running around in their underwear, no uniform on whatsoever. We're in the middle of combat zone, a hotbed of the Taliban, and these guys were strutting around like they were at a college frat house. I was very concerned.

It was frustrating to me to come in and see an American unit sitting on its hands. My point of view was that if the United States was not operating in an area in Afghanistan, then the Taliban was. If there's a power vacuum, somebody's going to fill it. The Taliban was operating almost freely in the area.

Before I took command, someone had placed an order for a new tent. It arrived when I did. I knew what to do with it. "Look, the first half of the tent needs to be a command post," I ordered. "Then we'll put a plywood wall there, with a door. The second half needs to be sleeping quarters for the command team and for the headquarters element of the platoon."

For the first time ever, the platoon finally got a command post, and it was well equipped. The radio now had a suitable home. We put a big map on the wall, and the men seemed to finally feel like a legitimate fighting unit. That was very important to me.

The platoon didn't love every choice I made. I saw canvas stretched on the guard towers, and I made myself very unpopular by making the troops rip that canvas down. I asked them, "How can you see the enemy?" Well, their response was, "They can't see us, so they can't shoot at us, sir."

"Hell no," I said. "We're not just going to let them have the advantage. If you give them freedom of movement like that, they will launch bigger and better coordinated attacks. If they're out there, I want to see them and kill them." That platoon had just completely given up on trying to fight the war, which put them in even more danger.

When a new officer took over command, the Taliban knew about it. We had members of the Afghan army and police right there on our base, and if they knew about it, the Taliban knew about it. This made it more imperative to show them that they could not come in and push us around, as they had been doing. That kind of strength deters them and saves American lives.

We rifled through the UAV boxes the first day. The soldiers came through and cobbled together a working system from the parts inside. It was an AeroVironment RQ-20 Puma, the kind of drone an infantryman can love. It's so small you can launch it by hand. The battery-powered craft, with a 10-foot wingspan, can go nine miles and perform surveillance with an electro-optical and infrared camera.

My arrival was a huge shock to the platoon sergeant,

who had been the de facto leader for a long time. He took offense to me coming in with all this stuff. He coped by sleeping all the time. It was rare to see him awake. Another young sergeant was pulling his slack by doing everything that the platoon sergeant was supposed to be doing.

The only immediate change I confronted the platoon sergeant about was soldiers not wearing their gear. I saw soldiers without helmets or bulletproof armor when they were in the towers. I changed that immediately.

For the rest of the changes, I appealed to him quietly. "Look," I said, "Uniforms are your lane. I'm an officer, you're the platoon sergeant. But I'm just telling you, the first sergeant complained to me that this platoon is never in uniform. It sends the wrong signal to our chain of command that we don't know what the hell we're doing down here."

He just shrugged it off.

I had conflict from higher up, too. My company commander, Captain Patrick Swanson, rarely went out on patrol. It seemed like he was hiding his hooch. It was up to his lieutenants to be seen in combat, and we filled that role well.

I've never liked bullies. I never liked the cool kids in school. When there was somebody sitting by themselves in the lunchroom, a little nerdy, geeky kid with glasses and long hair who nobody wanted to sit with, I had always been the guy to go sit with him because I just don't think it's right. A lot of that comes from the way my family raised me.

I saw that there were a lot of jock quarterback types in charge of the 82nd Airborne. The way they acted reminded me of high school. Swanson was one of those guys. I knew immediately that I was going to clash with him. I just knew that he was going to send me on some dumbass, harebrained mission that he didn't even understand himself. In that, he didn't disappoint.

For my first patrol, Swanson wanted me to take a foot patrol to verify that a certain road existed. His plan called for walking through minefields to reach the road, as if risking our lives to touch it was the only way to prove it was there. Swanson told me: "Here's the plan. I want you to do this at this time." He was trying to plan my patrols. That was my job.

"Sir," I said. "I don't need you planning my patrols for me. I know what I'm doing. I know what you want done in your area. If you're going to micromanage, then you might as well just give me another job because I'm not going to do this one."

I think that got us off on the wrong foot. "Okay, sir, I'll verify that the road exists," I added. "And I'll get you the condition of the road."

After that conversation, my platoon sergeant started making preparation for the foot patrol. "Sergeant, what are you doing?" I asked.

"Well, looks like we've got to go out, sir."

"We're not doing that fucking mission," I said. "We have a UAV with a camera on it. We are not going out there and traipsing around just to verify that a road is there."

A big grin spread over his face, and he went to get the UAV. We had all this technology at our disposal, but nobody was using it because they were not thinking outside the box. But now we were thinking outside the box.

We launched the Puma from inside the walls of the strong point. The operator controlled it with a touch-pad. He flew the drone out to the objective, and lo and behold, it gave us a perfect video of the road. I crafted a report based on the video.

That night, Swanson asked me what happened. "I

notice I didn't hear you call in that you ever went on a mission today," he said.

"Oh, we went on a mission, sir. We just went on an aerial recon," I replied. "That Puma that we pieced together works just fine. It has a great camera on it." I gave him the report, complete with all the details. The look on his face showed that he knew he had been out-maneuvered and he didn't like it.

My NCOs asked me how often I planned on going on patrols. "You know, you don't have to go on every one," they'd say.

"Yes, I do," I'd always respond. "If my troopers are outside the wire, I'm out there with them. That's not up for debate or discussion."

If somebody that I was in command of was in harm's way, I needed to be in harm's way too. I couldn't ask them to be out there by themselves.

The next day, Swanson wanted another patrol, and there was no drone that could fill our role.

LANES OF BABY POWDER

The following morning, the first time I woke up at Pay-enzai, we went on our first foot patrol. It was very early.

The mission was basic: we were to go to an abandoned village to the north of the strong point to see if there was anybody living there. We had intel reports that indicated the Taliban were using it as a squatting position from which to launch attacks on our base and on other bases. We were going up there just to see if any Taliban were there.

A lot of people in the unit complained that we were wasting our time, that the missions didn't make any sense and soldiers were losing their legs for no reason. They saw no overall objective. I couldn't blame them. This patrol to the village was a prime example of a stupid mission.

We were just supposed to walk to the village, see if anybody was there, and walk back. That's it. Even if they were there, they would not still be there by the time we arrived. We moved slow and made a lot of noise. We didn't move stealthily. We weren't Special Forces.

Wherever we walked outside the Dorito, we were plodding through minefields. Everyone had baby or foot powder tucked into little cuffs on their belts. Every couple of steps, whoever was on point would sprinkle a little bit of baby powder on the ground to the left and right. That made lanes for everybody to walk in that had been cleared by a metal detector.

That left us walking in a straight single-file line, with a near-total lack of maneuverability. You *don't* step outside the lane of baby powder. This process was slow and obvious, and it invited attacks at the time and place of the Taliban's choosing.

We were fighting in a different way than the Taliban was fighting. The Taliban didn't move like us; they knew where all the mines were and could do all kinds of maneuvering. They were fighting in an adult way, as if to tell us, "We know what we're doing. This is our house." We were acting like toddlers; we could only walk so fast and understand so much.

As a leader, it's always important to figuratively stay in your lane and not micromanage every aspect of mission planning. As a new lieutenant, this is even more important since your NCOs have probably been in the area of operations longer and know the troops better.

There were three squad leaders, each responsible for about 12 troops. Each squad leader is a staff sergeant or a senior sergeant. They had operational command and control over their squads. I told them, "Look, I won't take charge of the element until it requires more than a squad, such as when we get attacked and we need the rest of the platoon to support us. Since I'm the platoon leader, then I'll be in charge of it. But until that time, as the squad leader, you're in operational control over your squad, and I'm just tagging along with you. When we get to the objective or run into anybody, then I'll take charge. It's your squad, so you get us there and get us back. I don't care what route we take. Just make it happen."

I had the ultimate authority or the approval authority, but they chose the route. I had just gotten there. Although they had been pulled off the line for a few days, before that, they had been in Payenzai for some time, so these guys were more familiar with the area than I was.

That didn't stop people from later complaining during my court-martial about the difficulty of the routes we took. I didn't choose those routes because it was standard practice and smart leadership not to.

One of the things that we in the military say all the time is "Let people lead." You don't want one person micromanaging everything. My job as a platoon leader was to let my NCOs do their job. I'd let them lead their troops, but I'd make sure I was double-checking. I would perform spot checks here and there. Every once in a while, I would go up to a random guy and tug on his canteen case to see if it was full or examine a soldier's magazine to see if there were rounds in it. It was not my job to inspect every single soldier, but it *was* my job to make sure that the NCOs were doing their jobs.

The NCOs track, on a very detailed level, every soldier's individual qualifications, certifications, talent—everything. They're a lot better suited to make staffing decisions than officers. I would tell the NCO, "Hey, we need to make sure this happens," and they would put the right person on it.

Back on the mission, we slowly walked single file through minefields. All around us were structures that reminded me of the pueblos in northern New Mexico. Surrounding these compounds were fields of grapes, grown on similar earthen walls six to eight feet tall. These walls formed rows that you had to walk down, which was dangerous because it canalized enemy fire (which made it easier for the enemy to shoot us and plant bombs), or you had to climb over the walls, which was exhausting. We did not hump over every wall that day because the NCOs found another way to get to the village other than by walking down the rows.

We made it to the village, a tiny ruin with the usual battered walls and lack of roofs. Nobody had lived there for a long, long time, and there were no obvious signs of any personal belongings of squatters. Once we arrived at the objective, it was my turn to take over.

By then, the military working dog was extremely tired. I told the handler and squad leader, "Hey, find a place for this dog team. He needs some downtime so he can recover. He can't find stuff in the village if he's struggling to breathe."

My plan was to send the Afghan army squad to clear the village, see if they could find any clues that would point to anyone staying there, and then come back to our position and give us a report.

The Afghan army squad reached the door of the compound and sent a report back that they thought they had spotted an IED. "Okay, I'm coming up there," I sighed. I started walking in that direction, taking up the radio to update the helicopter on what was going on. My radio man, who was walking right behind me, suddenly grabbed me by the shoulders and pulled me back, cussing. He pointed to the ground at an explosive device, right in front of us.

"Well, shit," I said. "I almost stepped on that. Thanks, man." We shared a look that only two people who were about to get killed together would understand. He just kind of shook his head like "You idiot."

I had made the mistake of looking at the helicopter when talking to it. You almost couldn't help it because you could hear it, but if you're looking at the helicopter, you're not looking for the enemy. Learning that lesson almost cost me my legs or my life.

When we reached the Afghan army squad, they were peeking around the corner at the door and using the side of the building as cover. My interpreter said to me, "They think they see an IED."

They gave me binoculars, but I couldn't see anything definitive. It just looked like a bunch of wires sticking out of the ground. "All right," I said. "What do you want to do? You want to call EOD [a U.S. explosive ordnance disposal team] and wait 12 hours?"

He pointed at a rocket-propelled grenade (RPG) launcher. "Let's shoot it."

I thought to myself, *That seems reasonable.* It was his men who were about to go through the breach anyhow. I told everybody to pull back. The Afghan squad leader and I took the RPG and went into a field where we could get a good line of sight on the door. The RPG leapt into the doorframe and exploded.

Then I went back and was chewed out by the NCOs. They were upset because I could've gotten shot by a sniper. "Yeah, you're right. My bad." Then I told the Afghans, "All right, go clear the village."

It only took them a couple of minutes. Of course, there was nothing there. It was time to get everybody together to go back to the strong point. We started moving out, with the now-rested dog up front, following those white powder lanes.

We had reached the gate of our strong point when somebody started shooting at us. The NCO in charge of the movement got on the radio: "Everybody just keep going! Get inside the strong point and we'll return fire from inside."

That made sense since we were right there. We couldn't chase after the enemy because we had to stay inside this little lane of baby powder. We had just gotten everyone safely inside the strong point when the weapons squad leader came over to me. "Sir," he said, "You're really going to like this." He pointed to this giant 84-millimeter cannon that they were pointing over the wall.

"Yeah, most likely."

A couple of minutes went by and one of the NCOs made a whole show of putting both his index fingers in his ears. They shot the cannon at the location from which we were receiving fire, and the shooting immediately stopped. The shooters had probably retreated.

That night, I saw Captain Swanson. He proceeded to chew me out for allowing the men to shoot that 84-millimeter cannon. His issue was about "the law of proportional force": if our enemy shot at us with an AK-47, then we needed to shoot back with M4s.

It seems absurd, but there was actually a debate over this concept. "Proportionality is sometimes referred to as 'proportionate force,'" notes the military *Operational Law Handbook*. "However, the principle does not require limiting the response to mirror the type of force constituting the threat or attack."

Despite this clear, logical reasoning, ideological fights on the political and academic levels have cluttered the battlefront. In 2003, a Marine Corps major lamented the spread of the idea of proportionality. The fact that it existed across all the services indicated it was trickling down from the commander-in-chief. "Unfortunately, too many Marines, including a few judge advocates, misunderstand and misapply the law of war (LOW) principle called proportionality, mistakenly thinking that proportionality requires the commander to employ no more force than necessary to defeat the enemy and accomplish his mission," wrote Major Gregory Gillette in the *Marine Corps Times*.* "Not only is that idea contrary to maneuver warfare, it's inconsistent with the LOW. It is legal and tactically sound to squash the proverbial enemy fly using a sledgehammer in order to accomplish the mission."

Swanson may have been going on about proportionality, but in the TOC, I witnessed numerous occasions when someone would call in a Hellfire missile, ordnance from Navy jets, *anything* just to get one guy they had a positive ID on.

Major Gillette goes on to describe the exact situation my commanding officer was telling me that he would have preferred: "Rules of Engagement that

---

* Gregory G. Gillette, "Proportionality in the Law of War," *Marine Corps Times*, September 1, 2003.

confuse these principles might erroneously state that a commander can only use proportionate amounts of force against the enemy to achieve his mission. The commander acting under these ROE would be limited to engaging an Iraqi squad only with small arms weapons. Therefore, instead of quickly destroying the Iraqi squad using overwhelming force, the commander gets bogged down in a proportionate firefight with the enemy unnecessarily risking time and men."

As my commander reprimanded me, I thought, *Let somebody else shoot at us. I'm not going to be thinking of the law of proportionate force; I'm going to be thinking of how can we can kill him.*

At the end of the day, I knew I wasn't going to ask Swanson for permission. The next time the enemy shot at my troops, I would take that as a forfeiture of their right to breathe. If Swanson wanted to relieve me of command for killing the enemy, then he could do that. But while I was in command, we were not going to back down from the enemy. Period.

I knew that my soldiers respected the hell out of that sentiment, and I felt that they would always support me. No combat soldier worth his weight in salt would disagree. Maybe the officers in the Obama administration would disagree, but the enlisted men get it.

I hate to make it political, but at some point, this story is going to have get political because it was a very political thing, what happened to me.

There is a big divide in the military. Many of the officers in the Army are very liberal, and in my experience, the overwhelming majority of enlisted people are conservative. The officers listen to NPR exclusively every day, and they're the kind of people who say, "I don't have a TV; I only have books." I think that's silly because I listen to NPR, but I also listen to Fox News, and I find the truth somewhere in the middle. And I have books.

Many officers in the Army have an elitist mentality; they think they're better than everybody else because of their rank and education. That's how they see themselves and the world. They felt right at home when Obama was the president, that's for sure.

There are some bold officers, but most of them don't make it very far. It seems to me that to be a senior officer these days in the Army, you have to forfeit the love that you have for the soldiers under your command.

I had already been warned by my NCOs that

Swanson wanted to take one of our Mine Resistant Ambush Protected All-Terrain Vehicles (MATVs). I was just waiting for the moment, but first I had to wait for him to end his tirade about giving the Taliban a fairer fight at my troops' expense.

We had three MATVs at the strong point. They were the answer to the insurgents' use of explosive devices against U.S. patrol vehicles. They are beefy, four-wheeled trucks that are built to take a beating. They have V-shaped hulls that mitigate and deflect explosive blasts, engine fire suppression systems, and tires that can run even when flattened. Many have remote-controlled weapons stations that enable the crew inside to operate a machine gun while buttoned up safely inside the vehicle's armored shell.

One of the MATVs was our "route truck." There was a road that connected troop headquarters to my strong point, built by U.S. military engineers through somebody's field. It had concertina wire on either side of it. We parked the route truck in between my platoon's strong point and the company's strong point. Its job was to overwatch the road and make sure nobody started planting any explosives. That battle wagon was an outpost that kept our lifeline open.

The other MATV acted as a gate. It blocked the way to the strong point entrance to make sure nothing could get in. I had been thinking that we could probably find a more inexpensive gate and free the truck for operations. That's something I had been planning to do, but I didn't get the chance.

The last MATV was designated as our quick reaction force truck. That MATV sat inside the strong point, available at any time to respond to an emergency. It would also ferry troops back and forth to the company strong point when needed. Every night, when the platoon sergeant went up to the commander's briefing, he would ride in that truck.

After he chewed me out about the law of proportional force, Swanson finally said, "We've got a convoy tomorrow. I'm going to need one of your trucks."

"Sir, I'm sorry. Absolutely not."

"What?" Nobody had ever told him "no" like that.

"Absolutely not, sir. If you take one of my trucks, that makes me combat ineffective, and I can't go on any patrols or do anything. We'd have to sit just there on our hands all day. If the enemy attacks, we can't even respond," I told him. "If you take one of my trucks, I am combat ineffective."

Standing nearby, my platoon sergeant was looking at me with eyes about as big as beach balls.

"You realize I could just order you to give me your truck, right?" Swanson said.

"I do realize that, sir," I said. "But I'm not going to give it to you voluntarily. And if you want it, quite frankly, you're going to have to come down there and take it."

I knew that he would back down because he had the reputation of never coming to our strong point because it was too dangerous. "Okay," he said. "We'll figure out something else here," and then he made a childish point of trying to ignore me for the rest of the conversation.

When I stood up to him, he immediately must have thought, *This guy is going to be a problem.* He knew for sure that I wasn't going to be a sycophant that he could order around to make himself look good.

At my court-martial, someone had said that I had my own ideas about how the war should be fought. That's not completely untrue because I did see a lot of dumb things that the Army was doing just because somebody in an office somewhere told them to do it. I vowed to fight back, relying on my enlisted experience and on the ideas of my enlisted men.

When we left the tent, my platoon sergeant said, "Sir, that was the most badass thing I've ever seen in my life."

I looked at him but didn't smile. "Sergeant, was I wrong?"

"You were absolutely right, sir."

FIRST NIGHT

I'm a huge planner. Everybody makes fun of me because I plot everything meticulously. I don't feel comfortable embarking on any project without having a couple of plans ready.

The most exciting part of being an infantry officer is that you can make up your own patrols based on what you know needs to happen in your area. Most of the young lieutenants frankly are not prepared for this, but the good thing is there are a lot of NCOs who are.

I tried to make sure that my patrols fit within the commander's mission. And I tried to pattern my actions, both in combat and in life, on a book I had read, *A Message to Garcia*. Essentially, President McKinley sent an

Army officer to Cuba to give a message to General Garcia. The officer encountered every obstacle you could possibly think of. It's like God Himself did not want this message getting through. The only thing that the officer knew was that the president of the United States wanted this message to get to General Garcia, and so he would do whatever he had to do to make that happen. So the moral of the book is that if you know what the end state is and what needs to be done, don't go back to ask what to do every time you run into an obstacle because that's not being a true leader.

The problem in the military these days is that when people run into that first obstacle, they immediately go back to whoever gave them their assignment and say, "Okay, what do I do? How do I get around this?" Officers have such great technology that we can just pick up the phone and text or call our commanders. We don't stop and think through the problem ourselves. People are scared to make decisions, and it's easier to get somebody else to decide for them.

Colonel Mennes was very concerned and frustrated that there were paratroopers and platoon leaders who were refusing to go on patrols. The enlisted guys would put a lot of pressure on the lieutenant to stay inside the wire and wait out their deployments. A lot of the lieutenants were acquiescent and didn't leave their patrol bases for days at a time.

Mennes would actually sneak up on platoon leaders unannounced, just to see what they were doing. That's how pervasive the problem was. He felt that it was his job to make sure they were patrolling. He griped and complained about it every single night.

I had a good understanding of what Mennes wanted done in our area from my time in the TOC. I was lucky to have been exposed to his gripes every night. I told myself, "When I'm a platoon leader, he's not going to be griping about my platoon because I understand what he wants. I understand the commander's intent."

As an infantry officer, I had to consider the priorities of all of my senior commanders when I crafted patrols. You write the priorities of your superiors, from the White House all the way down the line to the company commander. A lot of them will be the same. That's how you decide what your own priorities are going to be and where you can take risks to further the big picture.

This avoids the specter of pointless patrols that sap

morale and put troops at risk for no good reason. Your operations should influence the enemy and how they operate. It's infantry officer 101. You have to know where you want the enemy to be and shape your operations to get them to do what you want.

Among the Taliban, with all their crudeness and lack of education, the commander's intent is usually pretty clear. The Taliban wants us out, and anything that can hurt us will further that goal. It's a strategy of patience and endurance, two areas of weakness in modern American leadership.

The plan for the next morning's mission was to go into the village and put as many people's biometric information into the computer system as we could. If we ran across any vehicles that day, we would register that vehicle by VIN and the owner. That way, we could track people.

My overall plan was to start getting as many computer entries every single day as possible because I wanted to start seeing that intel in real time and I wanted to feed data about what we were encountering on the battlefield to our military intelligence personnel. It doesn't help if you come into contact with somebody and you don't know who the hell they are. What does help is when you take the person's iris scan, fingerprints, and DNA biometrics and you start to understand movements of populations and relationships.

That effort would begin the next morning. I didn't get much rest. I slept for probably 45 minutes, and I guess I was weirdly inspired by Colonel Mennes's sleep pattern. I knew he only slept 45 minutes a night, and even though I didn't admire anything else about him, I did admire his tenacious pursuit of the enemy and that he also seemed always to be on duty. He was the kind of all-hands leader I wanted to be. I saw that he could do it, and so I tried. What I didn't know was that he would take 45 minutes here, 45 minutes there, naps throughout the day at weird intervals. I would sleep 45 minutes a night and then stay up until the next night. It was exhausting me, but I couldn't slow down.

THE SECOND DAY

On July 2, 2012, we had to leave by 7 am. I had talked to Jared, my successor at the TOC, and found out that the Army helicopters were coming on-station at that time.

A Kiowa was observing at elevation and an Apache maneuvering below.

I told the men, "We are not going to waste these helicopters' time. When they get here, we're going to give them stuff to do. We will direct them in such a way that their maneuvers correlate with what we're doing on the ground."

I tasked the birds with making a wide area recon, swooping in a big circle around our area as we started out for the target village. The pilots reported back to me almost immediately that they saw people amassing on the fringe of our area of responsibility.

Again, my objective was to try to get every Afghan there into biometric databases. But as soon as we stepped off, the helicopters started telling me what they were seeing, and the mission changed. The Afghans down there fit the description of the enemy, but I wanted to see how they would react when we applied some pressure.

I told the helicopter to drop smoke where the people were located so I could tell where they were from my vantage point. Once I was able to get a good picture of where they were amassed, I wanted them moved to where we were.

Because I was on foot and had to stay behind a metal detector, I wanted to use these helicopters to push the enemy toward me. If I had to engage with the enemy, at least I'd do it where I wanted. I wouldn't have to run all over the battlefield to catch them.

I didn't want them to come toward us just so they could run into a wall of bullets. I wanted to see how they reacted to our commands, how they reacted to the helicopters, how they reacted to seeing American paratroopers.

They reacted to the helicopters like they were scared of them. After the Apache pilot dropped smoke, they all scattered to the four winds. Most of them went northeast of our position, out of my reach and into the U.S. National Guard territory. Two motorcycles came directly where we wanted them to come.

It was working perfectly.

After having seen U.S. troops in their country for 11 years, there were very few locals who rode motorcycles around who had not seen an American patrol. They know how to act if they want to survive the encounter. It's easy: do whatever the soldiers tell you. You certainly do not approach them at high rates of speed, whether they're in a vehicle or they're on foot. Everybody knows this.

The Afghan army soldiers at the front of my patrol started firing at the motorcycle. I was thinking, *The Afghan army are not professional soldiers, but they certainly are experts in their own country, their own language, and their own culture. And they see a threat.* I had never known a legitimate Afghan army unit to fire at its own civilians.

My soldier, PFC James Skelton, asked if he could engage.

On my first day in Payenzai, I had sat down with every soldier in my platoon and interviewed each one. It's how I'd been led as an NCO. I asked them about their short-term goals, long-term goals, what they had done in the Army, what they wanted to do in the Army.

For instance, when I as an NCO, one of my soldiers told me he wanted to be a pilot, so I stayed on him until he followed through, and he ended up flying helicopters for the Army. That's what you do as a leader. The 82nd Airborne Division moves really fast, so I knew that I needed to get to know my soldiers when I had the chance. It's hard to do that on the move. I sat down with each one of them; I interviewed them all and kept notes in a little green notebook.

This exact situation is why a good leader gets to know the soldiers under his or her command. In that moment, when Skelton turned around and asked me to fire, I knew whom I was talking to. He had been a former civilian police officer and that gave him a lot of credibility. That made him more mature in my book. It made me respect him more. Also, I understood the training that he had been through; police officers are forced to make this kind of choice every day.

This soldier asking me if he could engage was not just any old infantry private. He was a private with some experience that I could respect. With his experience and expertise, if he was asking me if he could shoot, I felt I should say "yes." If someone with his credibility has decided to shoot, he is sure that his targets are not good guys.

Between him and the Afghan army soldiers, who had already started firing at the motorcycle, all the available information steered me to say "yes."

If a member of the world's greatest military, an expert in what he does, is going to ask me if he can defend himself and defend his fellow soldiers in combat, who the hell am I, the new guy, to come in and say "no"? Am I going to be just like all of those syco-phant officers who I hate and say, "Well, let's wait until he comes up and tries to stab us in the throat" or "Let's wait until he comes up and throws acid on us or drops a grenade at our feet" or "Let's wait until he comes up and we know 100 percent. Let's wait until he's shot at us a couple of times." No, I'm not going to be that guy.

I've had years to reflect on this. These are the things that you think of when you're trying to make a life or death decision. And you think of them very, very quickly.

First and foremost is the thought that this is a human being. Do I really *need* to kill him? The next question is "Is he going to kill my men?" If the answer is "yes," then the answer to the first question is obviously "yes." If the answer is "I don't know," then the answer to the first question could be "yes" or "no," depending on what the potential enemy does next.

In the field, I know there are potential repercussions to every decision I make, and I'm very much thinking about everything that could go wrong if I make the wrong choice. I know the relationship between the United States and Afghanistan, and the relationship between the United States and the rest of the world, is important. So, you think, "If I authorize my men to take a life, will it affect that relationship? Am I going to start an international incident?"

The very *last* thing I was thinking of were the rules of engagement. My country had trained me for years to be a professional decision maker. They could train a monkey to go to Afghanistan and follow the rules of engagement. Instead, they trained me to make the best possible decision that I could possibly make in the heat of battle.

But the Obama administration wanted robotic officers. They wanted officers to not make decisions. They wanted officers to call them, to let them make the decision. All too often, that approach has led to failure when the officials wouldn't make a deliberate choice. That's how events like the siege of the embassy and CIA annex in Benghazi happened; everyone waited for direction and was conditioned to be nervous about acting independently.

On that day in Afghanistan, everything was telling me that those guys on the motorcycle were the enemy. Everything. I wasn't even thinking they might be civilians. And as it turns out, I was correct.

The answer was "yes."

I did not know at the time I gave the order that the motorcycle had stopped and had its kickstand down. The three guys on board had gotten off it and were walking toward the Afghan army. I couldn't see any of this. From everything that I heard on the radio when I made the decision, I believed the motorcycle was still coming at our guys.

Skelton engaged the three men who had been on the motorcycle. He missed. At my radio command, a paratrooper in one of my gun trucks fired his M240B heavy machine gun. Two of the three men were killed. One fled.

When I arrived at the scene, a woman and kids were standing at the edge of the village crying and shouting. It was terrifying to see; one of the things that had not occurred to me was that our enemies, the Taliban, *have families too.*

I assigned some privates to do a battle damage assessment and continued the mission to the village. That's where I encountered the guy who had run away. I ordered my men to take him into custody. I then ordered my medic to patch him up, and we continued the mission.

Around the same time that my gun truck engaged the motorcycle, my second gun truck radioed that a second motorcycle was approaching their position. I ordered them to detain that man. When we started going back to the strong point, I walked over to pick him up. He was sitting on the side of the road playing with sand in his hands. "You guys didn't realize what he was doing?" I asked his guards. "He's getting evidence off his hands. Don't let him fucking do that."

They were privates; they didn't know any better.

Before we left the village, the Afghan army squad leader stepped up to me and said, "Sir, we need to get out of here *now*! Taliban." I looked around. I had an injured detainee, soldiers were all over the freaking place, my dog was tired, and my helicopters were about to go off-station. "All right," I told my squad leader, "Let's go home." He charted the course to take us home. I walked down the road to my route truck.

MATVs don't have a lot of cargo space, but we were determined to bring back the motorcycle with us. I got up in the back of the vehicle and pulled it up, using a dead lift maneuver, into the back of the MATV. The detained guy who had been on the second motorcycle was in the cab, and we all returned to the strong point.

At that point, we used a test kit to examine both of the detainees' hands for gunpowder and explosive residue. The test is easy to perform and results are immediate. Their hands are rubbed with a solution and then stuck in a container and the result comes out. It's like some crap you see on *CSI*.

The detainee came up positive for explosives. No surprise there. So did the other guy who my other element on the west end of the village had encountered and shot. These were bad hombres. As for the two dead insurgents, their hands were never tested for explosive residue because their bodies were carted away by Afghans to give them an immediate burial, according to Islamic custom.

I told my troops to get the two detainees food and water, put them in the shade, and separate them so they couldn't get their stories straight. I got on the radio and called in to the commander, who had to be woken up, and he told me to bring them to his headquarters.

I went on the first truck up, and there I started the paperwork. Shootings are usually very procedural. If no Afghans come forward to complain, the incident just gets logged in the combat log: "Engaged two enemy and killed one." That's it. Everybody goes on about their business.

According to standing operating procedure (SOP), I needed to get our sworn statements done and present the package to the commander for him to review before he could submit it up the chain. When we arrived, I found a computer and a military intelligence lieutenant and got to work. I was there, typing on the computer, when Swanson came in and said, "Ah, do you have a moment?"

He just started walking and I followed. We wound up inside the weightlifting tent. "You need to know that a civilian went into the district center and reported that you killed one of their family members."

"Well, that's got to be wrong, sir. That can't be right."

"Well, you're under suspension until we can figure out what's going to happen," Swanson replied. "You're not to talk to anybody in your platoon."

I asked if I was being accused of doing something wrong and whether I was in trouble. He downplayed it and called it "normal procedure."

True to form, Swanson didn't ask me what happened on the patrol. Not once, not ever.

MANUFACTURED CRIME

It was a lie that any Afghans complained about the shooting. Here's what happened.

PFC Skelton felt like he had made the wrong decision. He regretted that his actions had resulted in the taking of a human life, and I get that. It's always a big deal. He immediately went up to the company commander and told Swanson that he thought that we had committed a crime, that we shot civilians. This was ironic, given that he was the guy who had made the assessment and requested to fire in the first place.

When I supported his decision, though, it became my call.

Soldiers are told all the time, and it's in the Uniform Code of Military Justice, that if an order is plain wrong, don't follow it. If a colonel, general, or even the president gives an order that is illegal, immoral, or unethical, soldiers do not have to blindly follow it. That decision-making ability is what being a U.S. Army officer is supposed to be about.

If I were a company commander and somebody

came to me and reported a bad shooting, I probably would call in the people involved and ask what happened. I'd want to hear their side of the story. But Swanson didn't do that.

He called everybody else he could think of, because he thought he was doing what command wanted. But the sad part is that he didn't exhibit any leadership. All he did was pass on information. He didn't do any investigating; he just jumped on one side of the bandwagon.

If anyone had interviewed me and found I was crazy and just wanted to kill people, then of course I should've been thrown in jail. But no one interviewed me. If they had actually interviewed me, they would have seen that I tried to make the best decision I could possibly make in a terrible situation. When you make a decision in good faith, even if it's the wrong decision, I think it's completely different than making the same decision in bad faith. I made the decision in good faith. I thought I was doing the right thing. If I have soldiers who do that, I'm going to do everything I can to stand behind them. Maybe that makes me different than most of the cowards who are leading the military these days.

Instead, the wheels of justice started turning so

quickly, and at such a high command level, that the situation gained a life of its own. In the end, they manufactured a crime when there was none.

There was a culture in the military at the time, coming from the top down, where reporting something against the United States was the biggest sort of accolade. Delivering a soldier on a murder charge would give the Obama administration something to tell the Karzai government when it complained about our presence in Afghanistan. Holding your troops accountable would get you on the colonel's radar. We were not nearly as afraid of the Taliban as we were of a knife to the back. Most of the time when you were on the colonel's radar, it was in a bad way, and everybody wanted to be on Mennes's radar in a good way.

How would touting a civilian shooting *help* diplomacy? At that time, the situation was in flux. Obama was hosting NATO in Chicago in late May 2012. The leaders of the NATO member countries were on track to endorse an "exit strategy" for the war in Afghanistan and, at the same time, claim a "long-term commitment" to the nation.

One obstacle was the corrupt government in Kabul. President Karzai had been calling for a review of the presence of all foreign forces in Afghanistan since 2008.

Karzai wanted to try American troops in an Afghan court, and even the Obama Pentagon knew that was a horrible idea. Over the years, Karzai had used civilian casualties as leverage in negotiations. This was even more true in 2012, as the White House signaled it was ready to change the paperwork that legally grounded the war. That's when Robert Bales shot and killed 16 people in a door-to-door massacre that made headlines.

In 2012, the Congressional Research Service noted: "The deadly attacks on Afghan civilians allegedly by a U.S. servicemember have raised questions regarding the Status of Forces Agreement (SOFA) in place between the United States and Afghanistan that would govern whether Afghan law would apply in this circumstance. SOFAs are multilateral or bilateral agreements that generally establish the framework under which U.S. military personnel operate in a foreign country and how domestic laws of the foreign jurisdiction apply toward U.S. personnel in that country."[*]

The Obama administration needed to make the Afghan government think that the United States had control over its own affairs. In return, they would get

---

[*] R. Chuck Maso, "Status of Forces Agreement (SOFA): What Is It, and How Has It Been Utilized?" Congressional Research Service, March 15, 2012.

an acceptable, new SOFA. President Karzai would look good to his people because he held the United States accountable and at the same time appear to cooperate with Washington, D.C.

In light of all of these benefits, throwing one soldier to the wolves seemed like an acceptable sacrifice. That is, if you're not the soldier being sacrificed.

I look at this big picture and it changes nothing. If I have to make a decision that sends me to prison but sends my troops home safe instead of in body bags, then I would do it any day of the week. I would hope that if I have a son or daughter one day who joins the military that they are under the command of somebody with a mentality that sets the main priority as keeping soldiers from being killed unnecessarily. An American soldier is a human being, and human life matters.

WHEELS OF JUSTICE

I woke up later that night in a random tent at headquarters, hearing the battalion commander's squeaky voice. I roused myself to see what was going on and parked by a burn barrel. One of my fellow lieutenants came over to see if I was all right. "This looks like it could be kind of serious," he said.

"What looks like it could be serious?"

"This whole thing with your platoon today," he responded.

It was just a patrol. I didn't understand that I was being thrown under the bus even at that moment. I thought it was just normal procedure. Lt. Col. Jeffrey Howard came over looking disturbed. "What made you think these guys were enemy?" he asked. "What made you think that you could open fire?" I told him everything that had happened. It seemed to me like he understood and agreed with me. Little did I know that he had already sold me out.

Just after that, I saw my platoon sergeant arrive and head into the company command post. I saw the battalion commander asking my platoon sergeant to explain the patrol on the map that was on the wall. I thought this was something I ought to be in there for.

But when I started walking into the post, Howard told me to wait outside. As soon as he said that, I realized for the first time that this was a them-against-me kind of thing. Even then, I never thought it was a criminal investigation. I never thought in a million years that the word "murder" would come into it. I thought it was just a procedural investigation; I'd seen dozens like it.

They transferred me to the strong point where battalion was headquartered. As soon as we arrived, they took my weapon so the Criminal Investigations Division (CID) could process it. It was SOP, even though I hadn't even fired the weapon.

The next week, I was in limbo. I would go lift weights, eat an MRE (Meal, Ready to Eat), and then go back to sleep. I knew the investigative wheels were still turning because the CID agents arrived. I could tell from having been an MP that they were CID. They didn't wear any rank or nametape or anything on their uniforms, and they carried pistols.

Then they brought my platoon up and put them in an adjacent tent. I was told, again, that I was not to talk to them. It was really awkward trying to avoid them because it was a small place. They had called in another platoon to take my platoon's spot on the line. I knew things were getting serious because we had just gotten back out there. *Okay*, I said to myself, *these people are overreacting. What the hell is going on?*

Division sent an MP major down to lead the

investigation. He seemed flimsy. I had been told that he was the investigating officer and that, at some point, he would want to talk to me. I watched him bring in my soldiers one at a time for interviews. Nobody was asking me anything.

I'm not the beat-around-the-bush type, so I just stepped into his path one day. "Sir, do you want to interview me?"

"Yeah, I'll get to you," he replied. He never interviewed me, ever. He crafted his report and made his recommendation (which I have never seen, but it could not have been good for me) with no input from me.

Even worse, before we left the command patrol base, I had seen my soldiers being led into the dining tent. They sat around a table and the company executive officer, Lieutenant Tinsley, put paperwork in front of them. They were literally all getting on the same page. Somebody, I don't know who, told them that it looked like somebody was going to prison and that they needed to take steps to protect themselves. I didn't know that they were trying to bring me down to protect themselves. All of the soldiers were ordered to cooperate, and nine of them were given full immunity in exchange for their testimony—but only after they themselves were charged with murder and other crimes.

I do not think that my sexual orientation had anything to do with the chain of command turning on me, even though I know that they knew about it. I don't think that it mattered much in the eyes of the brass, but for my soldiers, it absolutely mattered. It made me even more different from them, more alien and more foreign. And that made it easier for them to make the decision that they made. Why would we care about him? He's nothing like us.

Eventually they sent me to Kandahar. I stayed there for several weeks. I really wasn't doing anything. Officially, I was working as an assistant to some major who was the logistics officer there, but he didn't have anything for me to do. "I don't even have enough work for me," he admitted. "Just make sure I know where you are at all times. I need to know how to get ahold of you at all times."

"Roger, sir."

I worked out twice a day. The movie theater there had a little coffee shop, and I would watch movies and read books. It was like a vacation, as much as you can have in Kandahar. There was a problem, though. I was not able to eat at the Army dining facilities since I didn't have a weapon. It's not like I could just go to a restaurant and eat; soldiers had to either eat at the dining facility or eat vending machine stuff from the PX.

At some point, I got tired of it and I sent an email to Guy Womack, my civilian attorney during this time, and asked if he could do something. All he said was, "We'll just have to bring this up at trial." He never did.

Finally, it was time for my unit to leave Afghanistan. When everybody started coming up from the line, they came to Kandahar to turn in trucks and certain equipment and get on the planes that would ultimately take them back to Fort Bragg.

When my unit got there, it got there in bulk. I went to the flight manifest formation to get my name on the list so I could get on a plane. Enlisted troops are told when they're leaving, but for officers, it was different because they might have other things to get done. If you didn't find your own way home, you might never leave.

I wanted to make sure I had a ride home. I heard about a formation, and so I showed up and stood in the back with all the officers. I planned on finding the human resources officer to make sure I'd be on a manifest. How else was I supposed to get home?

But before I could find the officer, I heard a familiar squeaky voice. "What the fuck are you doing here?"

I looked around, trying to see whom Lt. Col. Howard was talking to. Hearing his squeaks always made me laugh on the inside with pity. Not this time; he was yelling at me from across the courtyard. "What do you think you're doing here?"

"Well, I'm going home, sir." I said it loud so everybody could hear me. I didn't want anybody to think I was being disrespectful.

"Well, you're not fucking riding with me. Find your own fucking way home."

I just looked at him and walked off. That's not proper military courtesy, but it's also not proper military courtesy for a senior officer to berate a junior officer in public.

As I walked off, the executive officer came over to me. "Hey Clint," he said, putting his hand on my shoulder. "Go talk to HHC* brigade."

He was basically telling me, the colonel says you

* Headquarters and Headquarters Company.

don't have a home here anymore, so I'm telling you where you need to go in order to get home. He offered me a little bit of leadership. I would have found my way home, but it was good of him to actually step up right there and in the wake of all that nonsense. It wouldn't be the last time he would impress me.

I went to the HHC brigade guy. "Hey, can I get on one of your birds?"

"Yes sir, when do you want to go?"

"Just put me where you have space, brother."

BACK TO BRAGG

When I went back to Fort Bragg, I didn't know what unit I was in; all I knew was they didn't want me back in my battalion. I probably could've just stayed home for a couple of years before anybody even noticed I was gone. Instead, I thought, *You know what? Screw this. I'm going to do the right thing.*

I went up to the commander of HHC brigade and said, "Hey sir, I guess I'm in your company now." He immediately started coming up with things for me to do. It felt so good to have someone actually need me. When he left after a change of command a couple of weeks later, Captain Zachary Pierce replaced him. He had heard of my situation, but he was more interested in trying to be really good at his job.

When we met, he said there were a couple of other lieutenants reporting to him who were in trouble who had just dropped off the radar. "Look, you can do what they're doing, which is to stay home all the time and just let me know where you're at," he said when we met. "Or you can come to work. What do you want to do?"

"Well, to be honest with you, sir, I'd rather be busy."

"All right, be careful what you wish for," he said. "I'll support you in any way I can in whatever you're going through. But we've got a lot of shit we need to do here. I would appreciate you coming to work, being on the ball and everything."

I respected that. "Roger that."

I stayed extremely busy the entire time I was under investigation. It was all operations-type stuff, planning and executing physical training (PT) tests, foot marches, vehicle training, and weapons ranges, and making sure everybody met all their qualifications. We had a ton of equipment maintenance and upgrade projects we had to do to get the team back up to fighting speed, and I took the lead on many of those.

From July to January, I thought the Army was conducting an investigation and it would be over any day. But I am someone who always tries to hope for the best and expect the worst. That being said, the specter of a court-martial was always there, but I kept busy to keep it at bay. I was frustrated that this whole situation was happening. I kept telling myself, *I'm a good guy. I'm a good officer. I'm good for the Army and they're court-martialing me. It makes no sense. I'm the guy who makes the birthday cake for the Army every year when I don't even celebrate my own.*

One day in January, a couple of officers from the Judge Advocate General's (JAG) Corps came into the office. They went into Captain Pierce's office but shot me some cold looks as they walked through. When they looked at me, I said to myself, *Oh shit.*

The first sergeant came out. He was a six-foot-plus African American bodybuilder, probably 250 pounds. By then he and I had become friends, just like Captain Pierce and Lt. Ross Creel, the executive officer. We all got along really well. I especially liked talking to Ross.

The first sergeant addressed me. "LT, you know how

to report to the commander, right? Three knocks and you walk in and stand at attention, salute."

"Roger that, first sergeant. Is that what I'm about to do?" I asked.

"Yeah," he said stiffly. Then he looked down at the ground and continued, "Listen, sir, just do whatever the commander says in there and it'll all be over soon."

I walked into my friend's office and I stood at attention and saluted him, "Sir, Lieutenant Lorance reporting as ordered."

Unlike Swanson, I had actually had the opportunity to work alongside and for Pierce, and I respected the hell out of him. The captain had paperwork in front of him, and his face was blood red. I could see the first sergeant in my periphery. He was over in the corner with his hands behind his back, clenching his jaw. The JAG attorneys were in another corner, watching impassively. They looked like kids in a high school cafeteria who are watching their friend as he is about to play a terrible practical joke on some undeserving kid.

The captain started reading his paperwork, a script they had prepared for him. He read the charges against me: two counts of unpremeditated murder. Obstruction of justice. And lastly, charges "related to a pattern of

threatening and intimidating actions toward Afghans"
as the platoon's leader. I noticed the first sergeant shift
when the captain read the charges of using threatening
actions toward Afghans to me.

It was the first time, ever, that I had heard these
charges.

"Do you understand everything I read?"

"Yes, sir."

"Okay, you're dismissed." I came to attention, turned
around, and walked into an adjacent room locker room.
The first sergeant followed me but didn't say a word; he
just stood silently against the wall. I think they were
worried that I was going to kill myself or something.

I was pacing in the locker room, holding back tears.
It was all I could do to not cry, but I wasn't going to cry
in front of anyone, and certainly not the first sergeant,
whom I very much respected. After 15 minutes or so, I
just wanted to get out of there. I told the first sergeant I
needed to get some air. "All right, call me if you need me."

I got in my F-250 and drove to a nearby park with a
lake. Looking across the lake, I finally broke down and
started weeping. How had this happened? Then I got
mad at myself for crying. I texted Captain Pierce: "Sir,
I'll be back tomorrow. I'm going home."

"Come in tomorrow whenever you want," he responded.

I wrote, "I'll be there for PT."

There was a pause in reply. "You can take some time off, you know. I can't imagine what you're going through or what you're feeling right now. So, take all the time you need."

I was at PT early the next morning.

Later the commander and I would have conversations about me going to jail and other aspects of my situation. I had started doing mixed martial arts (MMA), and he asked me why. He thought it was for tools.

"Sir, I'm going to prison and I'm not going to be anybody's bitch."

He looked down at the ground. "Clint," Captain Pierce choked out. "You are not going to prison. That's not going to happen."

"Well, sir," I said. "I've got to be ready."

PART III

THE SYSTEM

ABOUT A YEAR PASSED after I got back to Fort Bragg before my trial. That period of limbo was a miserable time. My professional life was in disarray, my future was clouded by criminal charges, and the guy I was seeing, Philly, wasn't making anything easier.

One night, this pyramid of misery dropped on me all at once. I had intentionally moved to the town that was the farthest away from Fort Bragg but still within commuting distance. I didn't want to run into anybody. Philly and I were standing in line at the movies when I saw one of the people I least wanted to see. My operations officer from Afghanistan, who was Colonel Mennes's best friend, was there with his wife.

I wanted to leave quietly. Philly was able to deduce that I had seen another military guy. He's one of those people who thinks he is a full-time activist in terms of gender orientation. His stance is "Either you will approve of me or I'll force you to approve of me. I'll make your life miserable until you do."

He started freaking out loudly, right there in line: "Clint, what are you doing? Is this because you're gay and you're in the military?" I turned on my heel and left without a word, furious. Was he serious right now? Did he really just do that?

Instead of being supportive, he was making it all about him and his freedom to be gay. It's just such a narrow-minded way of thinking. It's frustrating to be around people who only care only about their own group's issues. I think it limits you as a human being and hurts your potential to grow. Unfortunately, there are a lot of people in the gay community who are like that.

I'm the exact opposite. Being gay is a very small part of my life. But with Philly, I was constantly worried about his feelings. Really, he should have shut the hell up and supported me because I was the one being tried for murder.

It was kind of easy to ignore the court-martial. It seemed unreal, like a storm that was predicted but showed few signs of appearing in the sky. Once in a while, I'd get a random email from my military defense attorney talking about something innocuous and tertiary. My civilian attorney, Guy Womack, was worthless. He wore a suit with a cowboy hat and boots. Even I know that doesn't look right.

I had known he wasn't very active, but I didn't really know what he was supposed to be doing. I'd never dealt with an attorney before and I'd certainly never been on trial for anything before, so I didn't know what he was supposed to be doing. Little did I know that he should have been preparing me.

I was naive. I thought that there was no way the Army that I loved was going to send one of its own to prison for doing his job. I knew what was in my heart when I made the decision on that day in Afghanistan, and I trusted that.

Month after month passed. The seasons changed, and then the calendar year. I didn't know exactly when the trial was going to be. Dates kept being proposed, but the prosecution, defense, and judge couldn't match up their schedules.

It had been eight months since I had left Afghanistan when, just a couple of weeks before the end of July, a date for the court-martial was finally settled. My entire family arranged to come from Texas to North Carolina to attend. I'd get my day on August 1, 2013, or so I thought.

COURT-MARTIAL BANDWAGON

I was in the lobby of the courthouse at Fort Bragg on the first day of the court-martial when an Army captain who I had never met before came up to me and said he needed my physical training uniform sizes. "Why is that, sir? You going to go buy me PTs?"

"Well, I just need your sizes, your shoe size and everything," he explained. "When they transfer you to Leavenworth, you are going to go in PTs."

"Sir, what the fuck?" He just shrugged his shoulders

as if to say, *I don't know; they just told me to do this.* I gave him my measurements.

This was the first obvious sign that I was going to prison. There was something afoot in the background that made me feel that the senior ranks had already settled my fate.

When the court-martial started, we filed inside and met the judge. Even though judges are technically required to be unbiased, they rarely acquit a defendant in court-martial proceedings. Many defendants ask for a jury trial for that reason, just to have a chance. Of course, military command picks the potential jurors too.

The judge looked like a fair person. She was a black woman, around 40-something years old, and very accomplished for that age as a full-bird colonel. I felt good having her as the judge—until she asked the prosecution how long she thought this trial would take because she had a soccer game to get to at the end of the week.

I could not believe what she said. It caught me so far off guard that I turned around and looked at my mom and dad and my brother Cody. My whole family was just completely agape; my brother looked like he wanted to go up there and strangle her as the lawyers agreed to cram as many witnesses as they could into each day. I sat there thinking, *Are you kidding me? This is the rest of my life that she's rushing. I could potentially get the death sentence, and she wants it over fast so she can go to a soccer game?*

As soon as the judge made that remark, I started to panic on the inside. This court-martial looked more like a kangaroo court.

My worst fears were confirmed as the proceedings began. This was not a trial, it was not a court, it was not a present-the-evidence proceeding. This was to be a procedural, check-the-boxes exercise.

"Over about a three-day period, Lieutenant Lorance committed crimes of violence and crimes of dishonesty," said Capt. Kirk Otto, who prosecuted the case for the government. "Lieutenant Lorance ordered the murder of two men." The fact is that I didn't even know the motorcycle was parked when I gave permission to shoot.

At trial, even the soldiers from my platoon testified that the motorcycle driver ignored commands to stop. After 11 years of U.S. presence, anyone in Afghanistan with a motorcycle knew what to do when they encountered soldiers—do what they say or risk death.

The prosecution said that I "knew" murder had been committed "because of all the steps [I] took to cover it up." They based this on the testimony of my soldiers, who said I told them exactly what to report on the radio.

This was no cover-up. What I was attempting to do was to report to the chain of command in an exact way. I had worked in the TOC that received those reports, and I knew specifically what they needed to know. There's a reason that resources are wasted on the battlefield. Saying something in a certain way on the radio can trigger unneeded resources and manpower. I wanted my radio man to say exactly what I wanted him to say.

It was extremely important to phrase things the right way so the TOC would not think we were in an extended contact situation. That's why I harped on the radio man, telling him to say things exactly the way I wanted. This fact just happened to fit into the narrative, the predetermined narrative that the prosecution had already come up with, that I was trying to cover things up because I was trying to tell them how to report things.

They did whatever they could to create the perception of a cover-up by me—a cover-up that didn't exist. During the court-martial, they assigned great significance to whom I assigned to do the battle damage assessment. When I first took over the platoon, I sat down with each individual, and I learned as much about the person as I possibly could. So, I knew that the guys who I sent on the battle damage assessment had the exact same training to do the intelligence gathering as PFC Skelton.

To his credit, I did not want Skelton doing the assessment because I wanted him right next to me. I wanted him with me because I knew that the main effort of the operation was not to do battle damage assessment; the main effort of the operation was to continue through the village and complete the mission.

Another tactic the prosecution used with much success in my court-martial was describing the scene of a woman and her two kids crying over the men we had killed. That helped paint the picture of these men as "civilians" who must have been innocent. No one pointed out that bad people have families, too. It doesn't make them civilians.

The military personnel from Afghanistan, from the 82nd Airborne, who to this day continue to defame me and say terrible things about me, don't even know me.

One of them even called in a bomb threat to one of my online supporters. They have threatened to kill my mother; on social media, one told my mother that "the day he walks out of prison is the day that I put a bullet in his head." The worst part is that I don't even know them. I don't even remember most of their names. I certainly don't remember their faces. They're obsessed with me and I don't even know them. To be clear, I vividly remember the men who were on patrol with me that day, but I hadn't had the time to get to know all forty of the men in the platoon since these men were only under my command for 72 hours in 2012.

I draw parallels between those types of people and the random Iranian-backed militia in Iraq. Some people are just going to hate you—they don't have a good reason to; they just do. Human nature allows people to jump to firm conclusions based on ill-formed opinions, random stereotypes, or what some leader decides. People will use these preconceived notions as a launchpads from which to defame you, and they won't stop. That's just the way life is, and you've just got to deal with it.

When I heard the sworn statements by those soldiers, I understood that Mennes and his gang of sycophants had solicited everyone for salacious dirt on me. It was bad enough that they made me sound like a blood-thirsty officer and an insidious murderer. On top of that, they heaped petty complaints about my character.

In one of his sworn statements at my court-martial, Sergeant Williams said that one time he woke me up and I jumped onto my feet like a madman. I remember the incident, and it was nothing. Sleeping 45 minutes a day and being woken up is disorienting. I said something like, "Where the hell am I? Why am I up so early, and why do I feel like shit?" In his sworn statement, Williams made sure to make me look like I was nuts. But in reality, I just wasn't getting enough sleep.

Williams had jumped on the bandwagon by stretching for material to make me look bad. And Sergeant Williams wasn't alone. There was a Captain Page who had nothing else to offer but that one time he heard me tell a female sergeant first class that she smelled good. That was the only bad thing he could report about me. I thought to myself, *You idiot. You want to be on the bandwagon so bad that you offered this random, simple anecdote. And the government took it to trial.*

Here's the backstory to that comment—not that it matters. One sergeant first class I worked with was a married, middle-age woman (and by the way, I'm gay). One day, during a meeting we both attended, she got chewed out by the major, and she was having an absolutely terrible day. A couple of hours later, I ran across her, and she smelled good. I saw a chance to help: "Dang, sergeant, you smell good!" She knew I wasn't trying to get with her. I knew that a good-looking guy like myself could make her feel better about herself and her life at least for a moment. And it did. She never reported that I'd offended her because I hadn't.

The prosecution led the jury to believe the dead and wounded were "civilian casualties." The Army did fingerprint and DNA analysis that produced evidence linking them to bombmaking. These guys had been involved in killing NATO and U.S. soldiers. But the jury never heard this—I didn't even know about the results of those tests until much later.

I also later learned that a civilian contract intelligence analyst examining blimp footage reported men "scouting" my platoon the morning of the attack. He reported seeing men who fit the description of the Taliban who'd operated in that area. My chain of command ignored him. So did the prosecutors, who never revealed this to the jury. Furthermore, radio intercepts that morning snooped Taliban radio communications reporting on the movements of my platoon. The enemy was talking about our positions, tactics, and weaponry.

My predecessor as platoon leader, Lieutenant Latino, wrote in a sworn statement that he would never let a motorcycle get near his platoon. This single sentence, and this sentence alone, was redacted for no good reason before the trial started.

The prosecutors were building the narrative they had been given, that I was an irresponsible murderer. My troops, threatened by their commanders and unwilling to stick their necks out for a guy they had only known three days, provided them with the ammunition they needed.

One of my attorneys, John Maher, later appeared on a radio program and summed up the inadequacies of my defense better than I could: "Another point here is that the Lorance defense counsel didn't do his job. Lorance's defense counsel should have found all of the [exculpatory] evidence…and then sat with every paratrooper who was going to testify and interviewed them with one of his investigators ahead of trial, which is totally lawful and is derelict if you don't, and I submit to you as a former soldier and veteran of Afghanistan myself, that had we slid across the table information that the army produced, that the people that were killed that day had killed American paratroopers and left their fingerprints and DNA on bombs, that those paratroopers' testimony would have been far different at trial."

What he said about my solders may be true. But I think they're all cowards. If I was in their position, I would have done the opposite of what they did. I exhibited this in my court-martial when they gave me the opportunity to testify and throw mud back at those soldiers. Being advised by my trial attorney not to testify and being assured, "There's no way you're going to prison," solidified my position.

The court-martial transcript has one sentence spoken by me, in which I indicate that I take full responsibility for the actions of my unit.

My mindset at the time was this: "If these soldiers want to come in here and say whatever the hell they want to about me, then I trust this jury to do the right thing and see through that."

They didn't.

At some point during the trial, I realized I had to become more involved in my own defense. I felt that I had to take up the slack of my civilian attorney. He had already told my military attorney that he didn't want him to do much, so he had taken my life into his hands. He should have been there on the ground instead of showing up the night before. Instead, he just seemed to wing it. Because he didn't seem prepared or able to determine at which points we could apply pressure, I did not feel that he was really fighting for me at all.

And I'm not the only soldier he has represented in this way.

I tried to steer my defense. When Colonel Halstead, the deputy brigade commander, got up to testify for the prosecution, I turned him into a defense witness. The prosecution was going to use him to talk about the effect of my decisions on the rest of the unit. My lawyer didn't know who the hell he was, so I slid a little Post-It note over to him that read, "Ask him about my character."

To his credit, my lawyer followed my lead and asked the colonel if he knew me.

The colonel said, "Yes," and then Womack basically let Colonel Halstead control the conversation, which turned out good for me. Halstead said I was one of the best officers he had ever known in the Army. It was a "wow" moment for everybody in the courtroom.

It is hard to explain, but I almost broke down in tears when the colonel said those words. I had to read sworn statements that were in front of me on the table to keep myself from crying. That was probably the most difficult moment of the entire trial. Here was a colonel who knew I was gay, knew I tried to get out of the Army under "Don't Ask, Don't Tell," and still thought I was one of the best officers he'd ever served with. The words Colonel Halstead and Captain Pierce said in that trial will never leave me.

The prosecution had people lined up to disparage me. This was when I realized just how early in the process I had been thrown under the bus and how my immediate leadership promoted the idea that I was an out-of-control killer. Once Colonel Mennes made his decision that one of his officers was going down, everybody did everything they could to support his decision. It's disgusting. Incredibly, Mennes didn't even show up to the court-martial.

All the people who I had actually worked with—the people who had the opportunity to spend more than two days with me—knew what kind of person I was and what kind of officer I was. They all stood behind me. But it was really easy for the guys who I had spent three days with in Afghanistan to turn on me. It was either they go to prison or I go to prison. It was just a simple transaction for them. And now that they've testified against me very publicly, they have to stand by what they have done, and they have to live with their decision.

The court-martial ended early the first day. I knew I was outgunned, and my family knew it too.

My entire family, probably 20 people, went back to my house at the end of the first day of the court-martial. My dad and I went fishing down at the lake, and then my brother and I went to the back deck of my house. We talked and drank Bud Light. We spoke of everything we had missed over the years and about how we really didn't know each other because I had joined the Army when I was 18 and he was 16. We got closer than we'd ever been, as adults, that night.

Every morning of the court-martial, my family woke up with me, and the women cooked huge breakfasts and made coffee. The first morning, they cooked a bunch of pancakes.

Like any family with kids, mine is extremely vibrant. Even in the morning, the kids are usually running around screaming. But during the three days of my court-martial, we would wake up and nobody would say a word to anybody. The women would go in and get everybody moving and in the shower, get the kids in the shower, make sure everyone was getting ready. The men sat on the deck, stoically gazing into the woods.

On those mornings, nobody said a word. It was like we were at a funeral home. We'd all just stare at the table or into a cup of coffee; everyone was just going through the motions. At a certain point, somebody would ask when we needed to leave. I would always give a time.

I had rented a big passenger van for everybody to ride in together. That way I didn't have to sign everybody in a hundred times a day. I could just use my military ID card. The soldier at the gate checking IDs would salute me. I would think to myself, *You're saluting someone who's being court-martialed right now.*

The second day was the same as the first, a kangaroo court taking shots at my character, distorting what had happened, and making sure the judge would get to her soccer game.

It may amaze some civilians to realize that the military justice system is so broken. Joining the military means sacrificing some constitutional rights, like free speech and due process, and taking on more legal responsibilities than a civilian. I knew this going in. But the system can be rigged so easily by commanders, who choose the judge and prosecutors, when they want a specific verdict. "The reality is that military justice can usually bend the way military leaders wish to bend it, regardless of the formal rules and systems that armed forces put in place," wrote Chris Bray, professor at Pitzer College in Claremont, California, a former U.S. Army infantry sergeant, in an op-ed and also the author of *Court Martial*.[*]

Well put.

During breaks, my family wanted to be as far from the courtroom as possible. We'd gather in the parking lot for cigarettes and quiet, frustrated conversations inside the van. That second day, Major Andrew Lanier, the same helpful major who'd put his hand on my shoulder and helped me get home from Afghanistan ("Hey, go over to HHC brigade"), came up to the van. He handed a bouquet of flowers to my mother. "Mrs. Lorance, I'm truly sorry for what you're going through right now." He wasn't involved in the court-martial

---

[*] Chris Bray, "Unjust: The Problem with Court Martial Reform," *The Hill*, May 1, 2013.

at all or required to be there. Looking back, I can say that nobody in my chain of command ever gave me any guidance except for him. And now he came to the courthouse on his own? It was amazing.

"GUILTY"

It took the jury 45 minutes to find me guilty on all counts.

In a civilian court, the failure of a jury to agree unanimously usually results in a hung jury and can lead to a second trial, but the rules are different for court-martial juries. If at least two-thirds of the jurors cannot agree to the guilty verdict, then you will be found innocent. However, if a death sentence is involved, the court-martial jurors' decision must be unanimous.[*]

Most courts-martial end with a conviction and proceed directly to the sentencing phase. Sentencing is called "extenuation and mitigation." At this stage, you

---

[*] Margaret Wadsworth, "Military Court-Martial Trial Procedures," *Nolo Legal Encyclopedia*, 2020.

have the opportunity to present witnesses and evidence to show yourself in a positive light. This is a logical time for the now-guilty defendant to plead for his or her life on the stand, taking the risk of cross-questioning for the opportunity to speak to the jury directly. In my case, that would require disparaging my troops as liars. It may have been a tactical error on my part to not testify, but even then, I refused to lower myself to their level.

They sentenced me to 20 years in Leavenworth military prison, the only soldier in American history to be imprisoned for murder who had never even fired his weapon.

My dad couldn't really hear what was going on because he didn't have his hearing aids, so he just watched my mom's reactions and took his cues from her. He leaned over to my mom and said loudly, "What? What are you crying about? What's going on?"

She leaned over and told him the verdict, and then he started crying. My uncle took him out of the courtroom because, in their family, boys would get beaten if they cried. Even as old men, when one of them cried, the other one would hide it for him. My uncle took my dad by the arm and led him out. That was the first time in my 28 years that I'd ever seen my father cry. It was such a raw moment.

My brother got up with a shout—"This is fucking bullshit!"—and stormed off and slammed the courtroom door. If the MPs hadn't been rooting for me, he might have been arrested. But they were likely thinking the same thing.

Philly, of course, was crying because he's a big baby. I looked over at him and he said, "I'm so sorry for everything. I had no idea." He had been making my life particularly miserable in the days leading to the trial, demanding that I spend more time with him instead of my visiting family. I think it finally hit him at that moment how serious the whole thing was. It was way too late for that; I was already done with him.

The prosecutor pulled me aside and told me to go say goodbye to my family. After that, it would be time to take off my uniform and change into those PTs they conveniently had ready.

I walked into the lobby of the courthouse and my family went berserk. My mom was going crazy. I hugged everybody, and when I embraced Cody, my brother, I said, "Take care of the family and keep everybody together." Cody asked me, "What route are they taking you to Leavenworth?" I then pulled aside my cousin, who's a deputy sheriff. "Don't let Cody do anything stupid," I said. "Get everybody out in that van and get them off post right now."

I didn't want my family to see me in handcuffs. I wanted this last memory of me to be in my dress uniform.

I saw Captain Pierce standing in the lobby, staring at the ground, completely dumbfounded. He grabbed me and said, "You don't deserve this." I could tell he was sort of in shock. I cut him short by saying, "Thank you for everything, sir." He gave me look like, *How are you being so strong right now?*

That's when I saw Major Andrew Lanier, who had given my mother the bouquet. He hugged me and said, "Keep putting one foot in front of the other." I can't stand it when people try to give me advice about being optimistic, like "Everything's going to be okay." When somebody tells me everything will be all right, my instinct is to think, *Go tell that to somebody who's weak-minded. I don't need to hear that.*

When he told me that, though, for some reason it stuck. It *was* what I needed to do—keep putting one foot in front of the other. I thought of what he said every single day inside Fort Leavenworth.

I was taken into a little room way in the back of the

courthouse, and a sergeant brought in the PTs. I asked him, "Hey, can you go out there and look for Lieutenant Creel and ask him to come back here, please?"

Lieutenant Creel opened the door, a look of shock on his face. I didn't need solace; I needed help. "Listen, could you take my dress uniform and take it to my house, make sure nobody gets it? Also, I separated out all my gear that needs to be turned in. In my garage, you'll see four totes. There's 100 MPH tape on the top of them that says what needs to be turned in and what doesn't." We were talking about more than $10,000 worth of stuff, and I didn't want to get a bill for it later.

(LEAVENWORTH) PRISONER NUMBER 93197

It was around 10 o'clock at night when I was finally all settled into my prison cell at Fort Leavenworth. And oddly enough, the biggest sense of relief swept over me.

Throughout this long journey of being in Afghanistan and working for a year while under investigation, there were question marks everywhere and a constant sense of uncertainty regarding my fate. The questions were all answered when I arrived at Fort Leavenworth because that was my final destination.

When I arrived at Leavenworth, I was finally able to breathe. I realized, *Okay, this is where I'm going to be for many years.*

Everything we do in the Army is about adapting and overcoming. That's what they say: "Adapt and overcome." You train and you plan for everything. But as soon as you get to battle, the enemy has a different plan. They're going to screw up your plans. Your job is to be highly adaptable.

So, when I arrived at Fort Leavenworth, that's what I did. I adapted. I knew I was no longer an Army officer and that I had to become something different.

It was sort of easy for me to transition into being an inmate if I looked at it as a mission. I looked at imprisonment as just another deployment—a long-ass deployment. I told myself, "I'm going to do this and go home."

The first place I stayed at Leavenworth was a small housing unit called Reception. This is where the officials isolate new arrivals from the general population for a couple of months while they get used to being in prison. It's located within a wing of the prison dedicated to any kind of prisoner who can't be placed in the general population. In addition to new arrivals, death row inmates and inmates with behavioral problems are also housed in these "special housing units" (SHU, pronounced "shoe").

Early on, they had a psychiatrist come in and explain the mental health medications they had on offer: "If you have depression, this is what we'll give you. If you have anxiety, this is what we'll give you." Then at the end of the briefing, the psychiatrist gave me a sheet of paper, slid it across the table, and said, "Okay, what do you want?" They don't care if you're cracked out on Prozac the whole time if that makes you a better inmate. I prefer exercise to drugs.

There are about 12 cells in the Reception housing unit. Jimmy got there a couple of days after I did. He was about six foot, and we were matched in size. That immediately got my attention. At that point, I was thinking in terms of threat assessment.

In prison, you have to learn to read people's body language and you have to be an expert at sizing people up very quickly. It's not something that you can study or decide to learn. It's just something that becomes part of what you do daily. When a new guy comes in or when you walk into a room and there are a bunch of inmates there, you must immediately size them up for your own personal survival. Our bodies, I believe now, have this instinct hardwired into them, and you revert to this animal basic instinct when you're put in these situations.

I didn't speak to anybody. There were probably six of us in Reception, and some inmates were very outgoing. But I wasn't going to talk to anybody until I knew what was what. I was just going to sit back and watch. And so that's what I did.

Jimmy's a very outgoing, charismatic kind of person, and people liked him because you can't help but like him. He's just a goofball. I realized quickly, after listening to a couple of his conversations, that he's a family man. He seemed like a good guy.

His was a really stupid case. Officially, he was in for adultery. When I first met him, he had a 27-year sentence. He was an Air Force recruiter, and he was fooling around with some of his female recruits. One recruit's mother found some text messages on her daughter's phone and reported him to the Air Force.

Jimmy and I started going to the gym together. He worked out a lot, and I liked that about him. We started going to the gym together when we were in Reception, and we just clicked.

On my second day in prison, a staff sergeant came in and handed me a memorandum that stated I had been promoted to captain.

"Well, what am I supposed to do with this?" I asked her.

"I don't know. They just told me to bring it to you."

So, I arrived in prison and the next day got a promotion. It was just the Army screwing up. That's what they do.

Eventually, Jimmy and I moved into general population and got a good look at how military prisons actually run.

The housing unit was shaped like a triangle. The TVs aren't at the apex points; they're mounted on the walls in between. There were two tiers, just like I'd seen in every Hollywood movie. We called the cells "rooms" because you try to make every effort you can to feel normal.

My cell was a lot bigger than I thought it would be. It was probably about 12 feet deep as you walk in the door by about 10 feet wide. It had one bunk—we lived one person to a cell—and a little metal desk with a stool attached to the wall that swings left and right. There was a stainless steel toilet and a sink, all in one. We made that our bathroom and kitchen area.

The cell had cinderblock walls and a concrete floor and ceiling. You couldn't post anything; the walls had to be completely bare. But there was a little metal shelf that was attached to the wall that you could display things on.

There's a culture in prison that tags you for being taken advantage of—or not. There are two ways to react if somebody comes up and says, "Hey, give me your cookies." (I'm talking about real cookies, not a euphemism.) One type of person will say, "If it's that important to you, take them." The second type of person doesn't back down and give up his cookies. I'm the second type of person.

I was tested the first week. I was in the library, and of course, as the new guy, everybody's watching me. Some white guy came up to me and grabbed the atlas that I was about to check out from the library, saying, "Hey, let me have that."

"Get the fuck away from me," I growled.

I was admittedly nervous. I didn't know what the hell was about to happen. All I could think was, *If I let him take this one thing, there is no telling what's next.* Like everybody else, I got that prison wisdom from TV. But it spread like wildfire that the new guy was not a bitch. Nobody else ever did that kind of thing to me.

On one of my first days in prison, a guard walked by in the hallway and saluted me. You definitely don't have rank inside. That's not all. My third night there, a guard knocked on my door. As I looked up, he slid a candy bar and a couple of batteries under the door. So even the guards disagreed with me being in prison?

It created a conflict in my head. I appreciated their sympathy to my case, but somehow that made doing my time even harder.

GAME OF SECTIONS

Every prison has its own internal organization. In Leavenworth, the power structure is defined by race. You have the white section, black section, and Latino section, which includes any other race besides black or white. There are generally between 20 and 40 people in each section per housing unit.

A section is kind of like a prison gang, but there's not a lot of criminal activity going on. Also, there is no prohibition against hanging out or doing business with other races. But at the end of the day, everything is very much about us versus them. Your loyalty is to your section.

Those who arrive at the Fort Leavenworth prison come from a military background where you don't see color, you don't see race, but as soon as you walk in the door, you see that the prison is self-segregated. You see the inmates hanging out only with others of the same race, and so that's what you do.

The prison staff is clever. They realize that there is no way they could ever understand the nuances, relationships, and personalities among all the inmates. They know inmates are going to establish a pecking order, and they silently endorse it.

Every organization has a hierarchy and a way to demonstrate it publicly. There's a system in place at Leavenworth that's been there forever, based on seating in front of the TV. Each section controls one of the three televisions. There are four or five rows, depending on how many inmates there are, of seats in front of each screen. The row closest to the TV is the highest ranking. The person in the center of the front row, directly in front of the TV, is the one in charge of the section. It's called front row center. If you're furthest away from the TV, then you're the newest guy or you're the guy nobody likes. Or you're trying to do what I was trying to do, which was to stay out of the way and just do my time.

The white section had four rows, and I sat in the back row for two years because I was trying to stay out of the politics of the system. The closer you get to the TV, the more involved in politics you have to be.

When the prison guards or administration gets word of some sort of grievance, they call in the inmate top dogs and say, "Get a handle on this, or we will." It works just like the military system, where you have one person in each unit who's in charge so you don't have to talk to 50 people.

The prison administrators don't control where you live or what room you're in. The inmate hierarchy controls that. When you're a new white guy, you just go wherever your section tells you to go. You can't just move to a new room when you want to. You have to ask the people in charge of your section. There's a lot of politics involved. The goal of this structure is to keep the peace by keeping everybody out of each other's way.

The protection racket is big. In other words, if you

mess with one white person, then you're messing with all of them. That's kind of the way it is. And it's the same way with all the other races. That keeps a lot of the new inmates in line—and the new inmates are the most high risk in terms of their behavior. They're trying to adjust to being in prison, so they're the ones who do a lot of stupid crap. You can stumble into something and start a lot of trouble for everybody if you don't know the jailhouse rules. It happens all the time, as I'd learn firsthand.

The second social discriminator, once you're with your racial group, is your crime. When you're a war crimes guy, you are the top of the top. It's all the perverse street credibility that a murderer has inside, but you also have military credibility as well. In a prison full of military guys, you're the one who went to a combat zone and came back branded as a criminal of war.

I was in a very small minority of people who were not sex offenders. It was very frustrating not only to be in prison but to share space with a bunch of child molesters. Even worse, the white section heads were sex offenders. But one of the things that I learned about life is that sex offenders come in all shapes and sizes. It was shocking to me to see people who I would never have thought would do that, like a 19-year-old, good-looking, athletic, charismatic kid who was in prison for a child sex offense.

At least I had a friend I could trust. As a Puerto Rican, Jimmy reported to the Latino section, of course, but we remained close. After he would have a fight with his wife on the phone or one of his teenage kids would do something stupid, he would come to my room and he would sit on the floor. We would drink coffee and talk about life. It was cool. It was the first time I ever had somebody I could just shoot the shit with like that.

When it came down to section politics, he was a lot like me. He didn't want to get involved in it. He was a big guy who worked out a lot, and those in his section were always trying to get him to be involved in the politics. He always declined. We got along so well because both our minds were focused on the outside. With him, the focus was on his wife and kids.

The thing is, Jimmy was a really nice guy. I had to stop him several times from giving away his things. "You can't just give people stuff and not expect anything in return. They're going to start taking advantage of you." He would always see the best in people, and I would always see the worst in people. So, we worked well together as a team. He helped me to come out of the protective shell I formed around myself when I first got to Leavenworth.

There was another, unexpected population that caught my attention. In the very beginning, I developed a certain level of responsibility for all the guys who were in for war crimes.

One day at the very beginning of my sentence in 2013, (former) Staff Sergeant Calvin Gibbs walked by with someone. Gibbs and I fist-bumped, but then he said to his friend, "It's all right because the L-T is going to get us all out, right?"

Gibbs was sent to Leavenworth in 2011 and is the subject of a documentary and, more recently, the major motion picture *The Kill Team*.

U.S. Army Specialist Jeremy Morlock received 24 years in prison in return for testimony against Gibbs and other soldiers. Another soldier in that unit, Private First Class Andrew Holmes, was sentenced to seven years in prison and lived in the room next door to me.

When Gibbs made that offhand comment, I suddenly thought, *Maybe he has a point*. We never knew each other when we were in the Army, but maybe I do have a certain level of responsibility toward these guys. That moment acted as an unexpected impetus to get up, stop worrying about my own problems, and try to help other people fix their lives.

First, though, I had to fix my own problems. Philly came to Fort Leavenworth to see me. He just showed up one night, uninvited and emotional. I told him, "Look, it's over. It's been over for a long time. Don't ever come here again."

He started crying.

"You need to leave," I said. "I just went through the last however many years of my life absolutely miserable, and you're not going to come here and make it fucking worse."

I kicked him out of prison and out of my life for good.

AN UNLIKELY VOICE
FROM THE OUTSIDE

I had been in Leavenworth for eight months when I received a visitor who would change my life.

In prison, I read a book by Don J. Snyder titled *A Soldier's Disgrace*. In 1953, an Army court-martial sentenced

Maj. Ronald E. Alley, career officer, to 10 years of hard labor for allegedly having collaborated with the Chinese Communists while a prisoner in Korea. The Army had intelligence officers on board the transport ships returning the POWs to America at the end of the war. Essentially, they told all the prisoners, "Look, we know that all of you violated the Code of Conduct, so start naming names or we'll put your name on the list."

The POWs were forced to write their biographies while imprisoned by the Chinese, and Alley wrote a magnum opus of more than 100 pages to antagonize his captors. In Alley's court-martial, the Army prosecutors simply paraded 10 men to the witness stand and asked them one question: "Did you see this man write 100 pages for the enemy?" Each man answered "Yes," and the prosecutor ended his questions. It was a done deal.

After I returned *A Soldier's Disgrace* to the prison library, I asked my mom to contact the publisher and ask them if we could put that book on our website. We were just trying to garner public support to try to convince the secretary of the Army and the Army leadership to back off their campaign to try to destroy my reputation. I did not have any faith, and still have no faith, in the military courts.

Don Snyder is a professor at a graduate writing program at Western Connecticut State University. He's a passionate left-winger. "I hope all of you wake up every morning and thank whatever God you believe in for the president we have in the White House now," he once told his writing class about President Obama. "He's bringing our soldiers home from two feckless wars. Let me remind you that these wars were started by men with pot bellies in Washington. Big pot bellies that they push around like wheelbarrows."

Snyder was outside chopping firewood when my mother emailed him: "I am a mother in Texas. My son read a book you wrote in the library at Leavenworth prison. He asked me to reach out to you. Please call me if you can. Thank you. Anna Lorance."

"My first reaction was to dismiss this as some kind of mistake," reflected Snyder. "It just seemed far too preposterous that any book I had written could have found its way into the library at Leavenworth prison. But the first sentence in the email was difficult to turn away from."

The whole time they spoke on the phone, he was waiting for my mother to ask him to help us, but she never did. Finally, Snyder asked her, "What does your son want me to do? People often think that writers can make a difference in stories like your son's. But the truth is, they almost never can." In the silence that followed, Snyder says he regretted telling her this. And he regretted it even more when she told him that her son only wanted Snyder to know how much his book had meant to him.

Amazingly, Snyder visited me. He was a very challenging person, who right away questioned my motivations for joining the military to begin with. He said I broke my mother's heart by joining. "I was hoping to find him arrogant or dumb so I could shake his hand and wish him good luck," he said later. "And that would be the end of it. His mother would thank me for making the long trip to meet her son and then she would start searching for someone else to help him."

He read the transcript of the court-martial and was outraged. "It's as plain as day what the Army did," he said. "The only question is why."

"I can do the 20 years," I told him before he left. "But if I'd done nothing that morning and if those people on the motorcycle had harmed any of my soldiers, I would have been in a different kind of prison for the rest of my life."

Snyder drove to Texas to see my mom and dad, and then drove back to Kansas to see me one last time before he went home. He convinced me to do a two-year-long review of the Vietnam War. He would send me tons of books, three to four inches thick each. I did this deep dive into Vietnam; the exact same things that we were doing wrong in Afghanistan, we had done wrong in Vietnam.

"I know this attorney," he told me during that second visit. "I went to his wedding a couple of months ago. He's impressive. I'm going to reach out to him."

The man he was speaking about was Lieutenant Colonel John N. Maher. He and an attorney named John Carr showed up at Fort Leavenworth within about a week. John Maher didn't want to talk about money, only saying, "I'm going to try to do everything I can to try to help you."

Mom and I were talking on the phone soon after and she said, "Hey, I've read about this organization called the United American Patriots. Do you want me to fill out an application and send it to them?"

It was a great idea. United American Patriots (UAP) got back to us very quickly: "Hey, we want to pay for your attorneys." UAP then linked directly up with John

Maher, and he basically took over everything. It was almost like he didn't have any other cases. I had a banker's box in my prison cell and at the top of it was my Excel worksheet and a pencil, and every time something new would get filed, every couple of days, I would stick it in the file box.

"Clint, he's emailing me at 2 am on Saturday mornings," my mother would say, happily. "He's emailing me at all hours of the day and night."

Colonel Maher went to meet with my mom and dad several times over the years and spent a lot of time at their house. He became like a member of the family. Maher also hired Bill Carney, a former NYPD detective, to go over to Afghanistan and do some investigation for him.

The work was paying off. The details of the terrorism connection of the Afghans on the motorcycles began to emerge, as did the assessments of the situation on the ground by those analyzing aerostat images and radio intercepts.

Don Snyder is the one who got the ball rolling for a truly effective team to argue my case in the courts and in the public eye. His voice, coming from the far left, is no less passionate about what happened to me than the most conservative pundit. "When you send an honorable soldier to fight in a war where he cannot distinguish the innocents from the enemy and things go wrong and you put him on trial, it is not just one soldier on trial," he wrote. "It is the institution of the Army and the American people who are on trial with him."

THE FLAG ON THE DOOR

The whole time I was in Leavenworth, I had a ridiculous amount of support from the public. I got more mail than anybody, except for Chelsea Manning while she was inside.

I would always have an excess of stuff that people would send me in the mail. The guards would call me to the mail window at six o'clock in the morning and say, "Do you want to ship or destroy these?" Some lady would bake me cookies and send them to me, and I'd have to throw them away.

As long as it was paper and it didn't contain anything sharp or have metal in it, you could get it in the mail. Whatever season or holiday was coming up, I would display the cards I received on the shelves. People would make these neat little arts and crafts, like pop-up books and stuff like that, and send them to me. I would display those on my little shelf, too. It kept me connected to humanity.

One of the first supporters to really reach out was a retired NYPD sergeant named Giuliano "Tony" Schiozzi. He was hugely instrumental in getting a lot of support in the very beginning. Tony and his wife, Denise, are both just really great, patriotic people. They would take an 8×10 photo of me with them on vacations and then take pictures with my photo wherever they were vacationing. Tony would then send those photos to me.

They really helped to spread the word about my case. Somebody had told the New York Police Department about my situation, and I was getting more letters, cards, and postcards from active NYPD officers than from any other place in the world, which I thought was awesome. They would also send me all kinds of paraphernalia that I was not allowed to have, like little tiny police badges.

There were so many people writing that I had to come up with a filing system or else I would not be able to get back to them. The rules say you can have a certain number of envelopes in your room. I got around that rule. When I got mail from somebody, I would immediately take it out of the envelope, record the address in my address book, throw the envelope away, and flatten out the letter. I created a filing system using those big yellow envelopes. A-B-C was one big yellow envelope, and then D-E-F was the next one, and so forth.

I was able to keep up with the letters that way. If the postmark said February 1 on it and I had it in my room, then I had by March 1 to get a letter back to the sender. That became my personal SOP. I had to do it this way because if I received a letter on Monday and sent a reply out on Wednesday, then I might get another letter from that same person on Friday. I basically had to make my correspondents wait for a month for my response.

A lot of my time was spent processing those letters. And so really, and I say it a lot, the people who wrote me, all the supporters that I had, got me through my time in prison because they kept me busy as hell.

I was releasing letters once every couple of months to all my supporters online. I sent the letter to my mom, and she put it online. In the letters, I gave people updates on my case and how I was doing. I didn't realize it, but I had a very upbeat tone in those letters. I received a letter very early on from a guy in Texas named Jon, who had four different types of stage four cancer. He wrote to me and told me he was inspired by the way I was handling my situation. He was driving himself from Dallas to Houston for a treatment, got about halfway, and wanted to turn around. Jon said, "I thought, you know what, if this was Clint in this car right now, he would keep going."

As soon as I read that, I said to myself, *I've got to keep myself together.* Every time I started feeling bad or depressed, I would think to myself, *I can't give in because these people are depending on me to keep my head up.* And it would always bring me back, every single time.

I had it easier than most people in prison because I had all those people behind me from the very beginning to keep me accountable. But the sad fact is that most inmates don't have that from anyone, anywhere.

Somebody sent me a 4×6 photo of an American flag. I defied the rules of not having anything on the walls and I posted it right on the inside of my doorframe. Right before I left the room every day, I would look right at it.

My room was searched hundreds of times and nobody ever challenged me on it. The guards are patriotic soldiers. Nobody wanted to be the one to say, "Take your American flag down."

DISPATCHES FROM THE LEGAL ARENA

While I was finding my way through the physical and emotional pathways of life in prison, work was moving along on my behalf outside of the prison walls. In December 2014, one of my attorneys filed pleadings arguing that I was a victim of prosecutorial misconduct. The following month, Major General Richard D. Clarke, commanding general of the 82nd Airborne Division, completed a review upholding my conviction but reducing my 20-year sentence by one year due to post-trial delays.

That same month, January 2015, my supporters created a petition on the White House website asking President Obama to pardon me. The petition received 124,966 signatures. The response of the Obama White

House was to pass the buck to the Office of the Pardon Attorney at the U.S. Department of Justice.

Meanwhile, the United American Patriots (UAP), a nonprofit organization that seeks to ensure that U.S. servicepeople charged with war crimes are treated fairly by the military justice system, embarked on an aggressive public relations campaign to win a new appeal for me. In September 2015, we filed a petition with the U.S. Army Court of Criminal Appeals for a new trial, pointing out that fingerprint and DNA (biometric) evidence linking the two killed Afghans to terror networks was left out of my court-martial proceedings. We argued that biometric evidence showed that one of the men on the motorcycle was linked to an improvised explosive device incident prior to the shooting and that a second rider was also involved in an insurgent attack. We also pointed out that a third rider was connected to a hostile action against U.S. troops.

These were not innocent civilians; they were men with the blood of American and NATO soldiers and Marines on their hands. We put the pictures of the American troops who they had killed in our appeals package; it didn't matter. The three Army lieutenant colonels who compose the Army Court of Criminal Appeals already had their marching orders and they did not include admitting that the Army had made a mistake.

During these legal proceedings, back at Leavenworth as a war crimes inmate, I had a certain status that I didn't want. I didn't use it for two years until I got pulled into prison politics.

I can't just sit back when I see somebody being treated poorly or being taken advantage of. I Just can't be silent. It was the way I was raised. If somebody is in a bad situation, then you need to help them. That's how I had to do my time, but it's difficult to do that in prison.

I lived up in the corner, in one of the most coveted cells, at the corner of the triangle. Andy Holmes's room was right next to mine, but he was getting released. I had asked the white section people if Jimmy could move in to Andy's room. You've got to be really careful with how you manage rooms. Whenever one person leaves or moves, you've got to have people to backfill that room so you don't lose that room and so it doesn't stay empty. You don't want your prime real estate being empty even for a few minutes because if it's empty for a couple of minutes, then a race war might start. Some black guy could just move into it and be like, "Come kick me out." And that would create all kinds of racial tension.

So that's why you plan several months in advance and make sure you know who's moving where and what dominoes are going to fall next. You've got to have all that stuff worked out.

The white section leadership told me several months in advance, "Okay, whenever Andy leaves, Jimmy can take that cell."

The Latinos had already worked it out and moved their people around. When Andy left, there would be about six people moving to different rooms as a domino effect. Andy's room was not turning into a Latino room; as soon as Jimmy left, it would go back to being a white room. I felt like the Latino section allowed this as a favor to me, and I appreciated it.

Even though the white section was also doing this as a favor to me, there were a lot of things happening in the white section that I didn't like but I was kind of turning a blind eye to, such as the might-makes-right type of stuff that I don't respect or appreciate. As an example, if a 120-pound guy is watching a movie in the fourth row and somebody bigger and more powerful comes up and wants to watch something else, like SportsCenter, the bigger guy just steals the remote, changes the channel during the middle of the movie, and ruins the other guy's night. It just isn't right.

That kind of stuff happened all the time, and it was absolutely disrespectful to everybody. I would talk to Jimmy about it a lot. "I'm getting so fed up with all this crap. I'm seeing so many people being taken advantage of and treated in wrong ways." Jimmy always told me to chill.

The leaders of the white section in that pod didn't really have any kind of clout or respect when it came to dealing with the other races. That meant the balance of power was off, even though we had more people than anybody else. Decisions that needed to be made in the general community would be made by the other sections. The white section never had any say in anything.

It made our lives difficult because we never got any perks or anything that the entire community was supposed to be getting. Nobody was standing up for us, and nobody respected us because of our leadership.

I grew increasingly frustrated. It all came to a head

the day Andy Holmes left prison. Jimmy came up to me and said, "Hey, man. The white guys are telling me that I can't move up there."

I went down to see the guy I had talked to before. His name was Josh. "I thought you said Jimmy could move up there."

"Oh, well, the other guys have a problem with that."

"Dude, you told me like three months ago that this was cool, and we've already rearranged all of the Latinos, and everybody's already arranged it," I said, starting to boil over. "This is not fucking cool. So, *who* has a problem with it?"

He pointed at a table where the eight leaders of the white section were seated. I walked over to them in a righteous rage. I lost my temper. You don't screw with the people I give a shit about. That's just how it is in my family.

"Every single one of you," I said. "I'll take all of you at once or I'll take one of you at a time, but we are throwing down *right* now!"

Then I headed to my cell. When you want to fight someone, you go to their room or they go to your room. That's where military prison fights happen because there are no cameras in rooms. If you get in a fight in the open where there are cameras, then they're going to lock the place down and do an investigation. It screws with everybody's quality of life.

Nobody came up. I saw that I had the upper hand because they had wussed out. I left my room and went to where all the white section chairs were around the TV, and I sat in the middle of the front row. I paused for a second, and then I got up and kicked the other chairs out to the left and right, away from the TV. Then I sat back down and started watching football. I wasn't really watching, though, because I was in fight-or-flight mode.

I yelled, "This is my section now."

It was the craziest thing I've ever done. I had no idea what to do next.

Jeremy Morlock went to the phone, picked it up, and pretended to call someone. He did this so he could position himself where he could watch my back. I didn't realize that until later.

"Clint, what's up?" It was James Robert Jones, someone I respected and still do. He was convicted in 1974 of killing a fellow soldier and injuring another when they tried to jump him and steal his marijuana. He escaped, but the U.S. marshals arrested him—37 years later. He'd been living in South Florida as "Bruce Walter Keith." The authorities used facial recognition technology collected when he entered Disney World in Orlando to match a 1970s image of his face to his alias's 1981 driver's license photo.

"Bruce, you have a spot right here at my side," I told him. "You better sit here right now and show everybody that you're loyal to me."

Morlock also came over and sat next to me, and I told him he had a spot there if he wanted to ride with me. I had to build my team. I couldn't just do it all myself. Plus, it's lonely at the top, and you need people you can trust.

I needed to demonstrate, without ambiguity, that I now controlled the white section. I told those two guys: "All right, this is what we're going to do. I'm going to go up to my room and get ready. You guys are going to bring the white guys that were in charge over to this table, right outside my room. Tell them they're either going to accept this and move back to the fourth row and be a nobody, or they're going to come up to my room and we're going to handle it my way."

The guys to my left and right got every single one of the guys who had been in charge, sat them down, and told them what I had said. Meanwhile, I was standing in my doorway looking down at the table, ready for whoever was going to come up to my room. I had my shirt off and everything. I thought I was a badass. But you have to show strength, or somebody else will show you theirs.

My two guys presented the ultimatum to all of the section leaders. One by one, all of them went and moved their chairs back to the fourth row. Everybody in the entire pod knew exactly where they stood on the social hierarchy, right then. A loud-mouthed Latino guy yelled from the shower, "And that's how you clean house!"

One of the former leaders did take me up on the challenge. He went to his room first, and he rubbed baby oil all over himself because it made him more slippery. Meanwhile, as if in a theater, everybody was on the edge of their seat in the pod watching every single thing that was happening. I was in my doorway, and the guy came up, but before he came up, Jimmy walked up to give me a warning. "Clint, he just went to his room, and then somebody brought him something.

It could be a razor blade or something, so be careful."
That's a true brother, watching my back.

Meanwhile, Tyrece Mullen was rounding up all the black guys to have my back. I wouldn't find this out until much later. Another true brother.

We had to make sure that the guards (we called them "cops") didn't think that something was going down. There was always a guard on the floor inside our housing unit, paying attention to everything that was going on, so we had to make sure it didn't look like what was happening was happening. The whole place is monitored with audio and video, so you're not getting away with anything unless you're extremely clever. If guards had known all of this was happening, they would've locked us down.

I posted a guy two doors down from where my room was, positioned so the guard could not see inside his room. His job was to watch for a guard. If a guard approached, then he would come over and send a signal to notify me. The signal was the word "diarrhea," so he had to use "diarrhea" in a sentence.

This guy who had been in charge before was standing in my door, oiled up. By this time, I was standing inside my room, facing the door. I had my shirt off and my boots on, and I was ready to go. "If you're going to come in, come in and shut the fucking door," I barked.

He looked at me and he looked down at the ground, and he sighed. "Fuck, you're big."

I could not believe what I was hearing. He inched inside, shut the door, and sat down on the toilet. "Man, I don't want to fight you."

"The fuck! Why did you come up here then? What did you think we were going to do?"

Almost as soon as he sat down, there was banging on the door and a voice calling out, "Diarrhea, diarrhea!" So much for using the code word in a sentence.

A second later, one of the guards knocked: "Lorance, are you in there by yourself?"

"Yeah, I'm just talking to myself. I do that sometimes."

After a moment of indecision, I saw her walk off. I had a contingency plan. If the guards started getting suspicious, one of my guys would go over and start asking them questions and try to keep them engaged in conversation so they wouldn't be paying attention to what was going on. So, around that time, one of my guys went over and started talking to the guard.

I pushed the button to open the door, and the guard

in the booth opened it about 10 minutes later. I told the guy, "Look, man, you're going to go straight down there right now, you're going to get your chair, and you're going to put it in the second row."

I didn't move him all the way back because I respected that he sort of stood up to me. He walked down and moved his chair, and then a couple of minutes later, I came out. When I walked outside, everybody in the entire place was staring at me. But I walked out with my water jug. Nothing to see here. Just going to get ice. No big deal. You had to be nonchalant with everything because the cops were always looking for suspicious activity.

I brought in a fourth man to serve as a front row "consigliere." He kind of looked like a white version of the Incredible Hulk. He was a giant man, and he was obsessed with power lifting, always getting accolades for being the guy who lifted the most weights. That helped me out in terms of making my position more secure. Also, he was a math tutor and a very logical guy—very calm and peaceful.

He was also a child sex offender who molested the math students he tutored. He was not my first choice, but the others wanted him, so I brought him in. They sold it to me by saying, "We've got to have one of them up here representing them. We can't have all murderers and war crime guys up here."

If you're going to have people policing people, they need to look like the people they're policing. That was kind of the rationale I used to bring in that one child sex offender to be part of my inner circle. If they don't see somebody like them representing them, then they're not going to feel represented.

One of the things that I had observed about the last leadership group was that they always felt threatened. In response to that, they would bring in more people to their leadership. But if you have eight people at the top, that's eight different people trying to be a chief. There's no continuity and no synchronization among them.

I made it extremely clear to my three other guys that if anything happened, it was because I approved of it. They would be gone the instant that they made a decision without talking to me first. "Under the other guys, it was confusing. Nobody knew what was going on," I said. "Nobody knew what the deal was because there were too many of them. We're not going to get bigger than four."

A couple of nights after the coup, one of the guys in

charge of the Latino section came up to me and stuck his hand out. "I just want to let you know that your section got its respect back now," he said. It somehow meant a lot because he was a gangbanger from Los Angeles who was destined to go to military prison the moment he joined. One thing that type understands is strength. Another is loyalty.

Of course, Jimmy was mad at me: "Clint, no. I can't believe you did that. You idiot." Still, he eventually saw that it made the Latinos have a lot more respect for him. Whenever I was cooking burritos or something, I would always go and give a couple to the head guys in the black section and the head guys in the Latino section, just because we were all kind of in it together. When the black guys would make burritos and give me one and the Latino guy one, they would bring one for Jimmy too. It upped his status, too. The Latinos didn't know how to deal with that. Eventually, they just resigned themselves to the situation: "All right, as long as Clint is happy, then everybody just chill out."

I don't know if redemption is the right word, but to some extent, I finally got the platoon that I was supposed to have all along. When I took over and became responsible for all those misfits, it was the challenge of my life to get them into some sort of fighting shape.

I grew where I was planted. I think that's a good phrase for my time in Leavenworth. I saw people in this terrible situation and an utter deficit of leadership. I wanted to come in there and say, "I'm just going to be the guy who reminds you that you were a master sergeant in the United States Army. You were a fighter pilot in the United State Air Force. Don't forget that. Just because you are here now does not mean that you've never done anything successful with your life."

The servicemen people think of as hardcore, like the Green Berets or Navy SEALs, are usually revered. But when you put them in prison, they can crumble. It's the most terrible thing to see these accomplished people, who've done so many great things with their lives, completely break down, not just as a man or as a soldier but as a human being.

Once I took over the role as section leader, I became more motivated and started remembering who I was. I got out of survival mode and realized that just because I was in prison, it did not mean that I had to stop being a leader.

RUNNIN' THINGS

My three co-leaders and I sat around the table and codified all of the rules for our section's behavior. We came up with a lot of stuff that sounds stupid now that I'm out, but in prison, it was necessary for survival and to keep the peace.

Before I became leader, the rules were ambiguous. Nobody knew what the rules were because they weren't codified anywhere. I made a change immediately; everybody was going to know the rules because they were going to be posted. I wrote them all down and had somebody type them up. If we wanted to amend them, there would be a process to do that. "They're the same rules we've always had, it's just on paper now," I explained. "I'm trying to bring you guys into civilization."

The inmates had already been following these rules for years and years. The rules covered some common sense, respect-for-others principles that a lot of people do not get in their childhood. For example, don't walk in front of somebody who's watching TV. The rules kept everybody out of each other's way; helped maintain the personal space of everyone in the prison, between the races and individually; and ensured that people did not step on each other's toes.

Another rule was "Don't go over and hang out and talk to the 'cops.'" There's a desk where a guard sits all the time, and a lot of the guards are young females. New guys will come in, just getting out of uniform themselves, and they see that Army uniform, and it's familiar to them. But what they don't know is that the cops are always trying to gather information about what's going on with the inmates. One thing we always tried to do was to keep the new guys away from the cops and teach them not to approach them with any problems. Instead, we told them, "Come to the section and we'll help you."

Codifying the rules made everything so much easier. Whenever a new person joined the section, I just gave them a copy and said, "Here, this is yours to keep. Make sure you follow it or we'll have issues." I'd say that over 95 percent of the new people did not have problems.

That's not to say problems didn't arise. Probably about a week after I took over, a guy was talking shit about our section and complaining about how there were so many rules now.

I told a couple of my guys, "Go get him and tell him to come up here. I want to see him." So he came up and knocked on my door. He asked, "You wanted to see me?" And I said, "Yeah, come in and shut the fucking door."

He shoots back: "Oh shit, what did I do?"

"Tell me about what you've been saying about the rules."

"Well, I just think they're unreasonable and unnecessary."

I slid the rule sheet to him. "Tell me exactly what's unreasonable. Which of these are new?"

He scanned the page for a while. "I don't see any new ones."

"Have you even read this?"

"Well, no, not really."

"So, you're going out there talking shit about something you have no idea about. This is loyalty is what this is," I said. "All right, you have a choice."

This is the most gangster thing I've ever done.

"You're going to take a physical hit tonight, and it's your choice the way that you take it. You can fight me in a fair fight, which you're not going to win, and you're going to make yourself look like an idiot. Or you can take a hit."

"Well, what kind of hit?"

"I can hit you in the face with my fist, or I can hit you in the belly with this." I had a pillowcase with a bar of soap in it. The good thing about a bar of soap is that you're not going to kill somebody with it. It will break up before it does too much damage.

He looked at my hand and looked at the soap. Tears sprung to his eyes, and he said, "I'll take that in the belly."

"Don't you cry right now. You should've been crying today when you were talking shit about your brothers," I told him.

I reared back and hit him twice in the stomach with the soap as hard as I could, and that was *hard*. He was grabbing his stomach and crying. "All right, you're going to walk out of here right now, and you're going to stop crying before you do. You're going to go directly to your room, and you're going to turn off your light, and you're going to go to sleep, and you're not going to talk to anybody for the rest of the night. Am I clear?"

They popped my door, and he walked directly down to his room, locked down, turned the light off, and went to sleep. For two or three days, he wouldn't talk to anybody. I sent one of my guys down to ask him if he needed any food and to check on him.

My guy came back: "He won't say a word to anyone."

A couple of mornings later, I went down myself and knocked on his door. He came to the door looking like he had seen a ghost. "Lift your shirt up."

He showed me his nasty bruise and said, "It's okay, man, it's going away. Don't worry about it."

"All right, well, let me know if it gets any worse."

As I was walking off, he said, "Hey, Clint. I'm sorry, man."

"Just don't do it again."

I did not feel bad at all for preparing that guy for that environment because he became the most loyal person after that. My guys would come up and tell me, "Hey, man, he was defending you today. Somebody was talking about the section, and he was like, 'This is the best fucking section we've ever had,' and this, this, and that."

I guess that gangster shit works.

In a wider sense, conflict management is absolutely paramount as a prison leader. You have to figure out how to solve people's problems because people in conflict will see each other every single day. There's nowhere to go. Most people do not go around trying to create conflict on purpose in prison. But you have to be very careful about not creating controversy or conflict inadvertently. You learn very quickly that *words matter.*

Conflicts arise often, especially with new inmates. And I had to manage the aftermath if someone did something stupid. Inside the chow hall, the prison has posted a quality assurance survey. There was a little box where you could put anonymous tips. One of my new guys put an anonymous tip in there about a Latino cop, and it resulted in a crackdown that got an inmate in trouble. We came to find out that one of the cops told the other inmates where the tip had come from.

I approached my new guy and said, "Look, dude, did you do this or did you not do this?" He said, "No."

One of the shared, common areas we had was the library, which had a little study room you could use. Just me and the new guy met up with all of the Latino leadership in the study room. It was like a dad taking his kid to a parent-teacher conference.

There were six Latino guys and only two of us. It wasn't the best tactical move on my part, but if I had brought six of my guys with me, the situation would have escalated. We sat down and heard everybody's story. What my guy was saying wasn't adding up, and what the Latino guy was saying made more sense. My guy, halfway through the conversation, blurted out, "Well, I put that comment in the box, but it was about a cop."

I blew up. "Shut. The. Fuck. Up! Not another fucking word. We don't snitch. I don't care who it is. You do not snitch on *anyone*. You mind your own fucking business. Period!"

I looked at the Latino guys, "Guys, I'm sorry. I got this. I will handle this."

Basically, it came down to him snitching. No big deal—just the worst possible thing you can do in prison. The Latino section was beyond pissed, and they had every right to be. One of my friends from the Latino section came up to me and said the other Latinos were "gunning for your guy."

I sat down with the Latinos to talk about it. "All right, check this out. We're going to handle this. We're going to let them, i.e., the two new guys, the new Latino and the new white guy, we're going to let them handle it between the two of them old-fashioned style."

"All right, how do you want to do this?" they replied.

"I'll take my guy to the chapel bathroom, and you take your guy to the chapel bathroom, and I'll bring another guy to make sure to watch the door. You bring a guy to watch the hallway. Two of us will be in there as chaperones so they don't kill each other. And we'll just let them go at it. And it's over past this point."

Not too long after, the top Latino guy and I were standing there against the wall watching our guys beat the daylights out of each other. They were really going at it. We just sat there making jokes with each other. At some point, the Latino leader looked at me.

"You think they've had enough?" he asked.

We went in and grabbed our exhausted guys. "All right," I said. "You guys need to shake hands right now. This is not continuing past this fucking point." We all shook hands and that was it.

A couple of days later, my guy told me, "I cannot believe you stood up for me like that. Nobody has ever done anything like that for me. I will never forget that. Ever." My response was "You're a damn fool. Don't ever snitch. If you know something about somebody, keep it to yourself. It's none of your business."

As long as I was there, he never moved up in the prison hierarchy. I made sure of it. In a civilian prison, he probably would've gotten killed. In a military prison, we try to keep things a lot more organized and a bit less violent. Because a lot of inmates are destined to be transferred to a federal civilian prison, it's better they learn how to behave before they get there. It will help them survive.

It was prison; you had to have control over people in a physical way if you wanted to keep the peace. One day, a guy told me, "Clint, you're a benevolent dictator."

"You know what? I'll take that."

BENEVOLENT DICTATOR

De-conflicting the TV was probably my biggest management challenge in prison. To tackle this challenge, I ordered a *TV Guide* to come in the mail every month so people could see what they wanted to watch and plan ahead. God forbid a grown man *plans* something.

I would see men on the phone getting yelled at by their wives for missing a show they had always watched together. "I'm sorry, babe, I couldn't do it. There was somebody else watching TV." Those little things affected people's lives so much. I thought, *You know what? That can be prevented.*

In prison, whoever held the remote was the person who had all the power. Before I took charge, it was "might makes right." A big guy could just sit there with the remote in his lap, and everybody else had to watch what he watched.

I thought that was unfair to the weaker people, so I instituted a TV schedule. We printed out a monthly calendar and stuck it on the pole that the TV was mounted on. It was an Excel document, and it had fields where you could fill in what you wanted to watch and when you wanted to watch it.

Anybody in the pod, all the sections—black, Latino, white—could come over and put requests on our planner. I would take the planner and decide what went on the actual calendar, which I would personally publish and post on the pole as well. Once the calendar was printed and posted, then whatever was on the calendar was what was on the TV. There were no questions about it.

I enforced it for the first month or so, until everybody got used to it, and then my guys started enforcing it, and then the entire section started enforcing it. It got to a point where all the brand-new guys, when they would arrive, would see it and would start enforcing it.

It became a way of life, a culture of mutual respect for every single person, even the lowest ranking.

This made a difference in people's lives. For instance, one of the guys had watched *Survivor* with his wife ever since the show had come out. He put it on the schedule, and he came up to me, after the first time we watched it, and told me, shaking my hand, "Clint, I just want to tell you, I've been here for years, and I've never been able to watch *Survivor*. Me and my wife would watch it every single week, and it's our thing. It's our thing. We do that as a couple. Now I can actually do it because of you."

I ruled by Microsoft Excel and the occasional beatdown. I created an Excel document that listed everyone in the section by last name. It had pertinent dates, such as when they were supposed to go to minimum custody. I posted it right above the TV schedule.

The whole group would know years ahead of time when a certain person was leaving. That way, we all would know to go ahead and put in requests for his room. Instead of fighting over a new room when it became available, I included a place on the TV schedule where they could also reserve new rooms. No conflict.

Another thing I had on the spreadsheet—and the whole reason for me creating it in the first place—was a college credit tracker. We tracked the number of college credits that everybody earned in real time. There was a pie chart showing the percentages of people in the section who were enrolled in college, had completed college, had a bachelor's degree, and had a master's degree.

It was a competition among everyone. I didn't tell them it was a competition, but that's what it ended up becoming.

The newer guys really liked this; the guys that showed up after I took over, they thrived in that environment. The older guys did not like it because they were just like "Why am I going to go to college? I'm in prison."

I tried to motivate these guys to compete with one another to go to college and one way I did this was by going myself. The guys knew I already had my degree, but I enrolled in classes because I wanted them to know that I was going to do the same thing so we would all be in it together.

We updated the pie charts every month, and every month, the numbers would increase just a little bit more as people earned more college credits. I began to notice people stopping by to check the latest numbers.

Inmates would show me their transcripts, and they

would invite me to come to their graduations. College was a big deal at Leavenworth, a bigger deal than I think in most prisons. They would actually have commencement ceremonies. Guys would come up to me and ask, "Hey, man, would you mind coming to my graduation tonight?" I'd reply, "Yeah, sure, bro, I'll be there. I'll absolutely be there."

If you want Clint to like you, you're going to enroll in college.

There were a lot of times in prison when I had to try to ignore what people were in there for because you can't see them as human beings if you look at their crimes. You really can't. I had to try to improve them as human beings regardless of their history.

Some would brag about their crimes. One of the worst was an Air Force guy who had raped young girls while he was stationed in Germany. He was a serial rapist, and they started a neighborhood watch to catch him. He was on the neighborhood watch, trying to find himself. He would brag about that and tell people that he wished he could get out and hunt more girls. He was just a terrible dude.

Those kinds of people, I would not try to help.

I learned that sometimes when you give somebody

everybody else doesn't like a home, you gain a lot more from that person. In prison, if person A decides he doesn't like a guy and person A is an influential guy, then everybody else in the whole prison of that same race usually follows suit.

Situations often arose where a new guy would butt heads with somebody initially and then the section leadership of whatever housing unit they were in would kick him out and make him a nobody. I did not think that was fair, and I thought new guys should be given a bit of breathing room to adjust to prison life.

I didn't set out to do this, but when I ran across people in these tough situations, I would bring them onto my team. There was a guy who was really being pushed around in another housing unit. They gave him a chair right next to the trash can. I thought, *That's the most demeaning thing; you're basically putting somebody with the trash.*

I approached him in the library. "Hey, man, look, I need to know what's going on in your housing unit."

After he told me, I said, "This is not going to make me a very popular guy, but you can come over to our housing unit, and we won't treat you like that." Two years later, when he was eligible to make minimum custody, he went to the staff and begged them to leave him in my housing unit. I could not believe it.

One of the people who had a really hard time was a Puerto Rican guy from Brooklyn. He was a hardscrabble guy, and he didn't take shit from anybody. The Latino leadership was trying to make him smuggle some stuff for them. And he said, "No, I'm not getting in trouble for you." He was going to pay a price for saying that.

I saw him in the chow hall one day. He was walking with his tray of food over to where the Latinos were, and they all stood in his way and didn't let him sit down, showing everyone around that he didn't have a place with them. I saw it go down.

He was about to turn in his tray without even eating when I intercepted him and grabbed him by the arm. "Come on, you're coming with us. You got to eat, don't you?"

Ever since that day, he and I were attached at the hip. It was a loyalty thing. He became one of my best guys in there, always looking out for me and watching my back. Sometimes when you give somebody nobody likes a home, you gain a lot more from that person. Everybody has something to offer to the team, and you can learn something from everybody.

I ended up with a team of misfits who couldn't go anywhere else or who nobody else would take, but that made my team extremely loyal to me. I didn't do that on purpose. It's just that when I saw somebody in a shitty situation, I helped them. I do not regret it.

The way I looked at it, we were all in prison, and it's not my job to judge people. If you were in there, I wanted you to do your time in the most productive way. Some of the crimes were disgusting, but I tried not to think about that. The only thing that mattered to me was that people tried to turn themselves around, to be productive, and to fix themselves.

The prison administrators seemed to like what I was doing. Guards and investigators would come by and see the TV schedule that I had posted and the matrix with everybody's college credits. They saw it all but turned a blind eye to it because they knew it was good for every-body. I really appreciated that. They gave me a little bit of room to help people, but obviously, I couldn't go too far.

One day, I got into an argument with a guy who, since the very beginning of my reign, didn't want to see change. He liked the might-makes-right way.

I tried to be diplomatic, up to a point. "All right,

I understand what you're saying, but it's not going to change."

"Well, I ain't doing anything different. This is prison. Fuck your rules!"

Now it was a challenge. I had to take care of this because I couldn't just let somebody openly defy me and let other people hear it. That would spread instability like wildfire. After they unlocked the doors after count, I went in his room, and we fought. He lost, but I knew when to stop. I wasn't going to hurt him badly, but I made my point. He ended up with two black eyes. The guards did an investigation, looked at the camera, and called me to the office. "What do you have to say for yourself?"

I told the truth. "I've got to keep people together and when people don't follow the rules, I have to do stuff about that."

"We know what you're doing and we appreciate it, so do us a favor and next time don't hit him in the face."

And that was that.

PART IV

INMATES AND PRESIDENTS

I N MARCH 2011, then-U.S. Army Specialist Jeremy Morlock pleaded guilty to three counts of premeditated murder. He told the court that he had helped to kill unarmed native Afghans in faked combat situations. Under a plea deal, Morlock received 24 years in prison for murdering three Afghan civilians in return for testimony against other soldiers. Two of the soldiers he testified against, Calvin Gibbs and Andrew Holmes, were in Leavenworth. And so was Morlock. Holmes and Morlock were both in my housing unit. All three in the same prison. I'm not sure who thought that was a good idea.

Morlock was Gibbs's enemy number one; they hated each other. I quickly found out that *everybody* hated Morlock. When I first met Morlock in 2013, he was in the black section because all the white people refused to do any business with him.

I tried my best to keep Morlock out of trouble. The staff would lean on me to try to keep him in line. "Stay out of solitary," I'd plead. "If you go down to the special housing unit, then I'm going to be up here by myself. I need you to keep your shit together so you can be my wingman."

That was easier said than done because Morlock had a destructive personality. While I was in prison, he established a relationship with a female guard. The prison officials called me into their office to talk about it. "Hey, can you tell him to stop? Can you make him stop doing this?"

"It's a two-way street. He's not only hitting on her; she's hitting on him, too. You need to stop putting her in this housing unit."

"We can't do that because then that would be like

letting the inmates control the facility," came the reply. I looked at them like, *Really?* Eventually, she was kicked out of the Army, dishonorably, because she was accused of sexually assaulting him. He was an inmate, so he couldn't legally consent.

Before I got to Leavenworth, Morlock had a long, troubled history while in prison, but I tried to fix him while I could. I tried to make him feel needed.

We fell out over stolen turkey. One of my guys was a very serious weightlifter, and he had convinced a new kid to steal some turkey from the dining facility. He wanted more protein. Now, anyone can make any deal they want, and it would be none of my business. But doing that to new guy was no bueno, since they had no idea how much trouble they could get into if they got caught. Years in the future, they could lose their chance at parole.

That's when Morlock decided to get involved. He didn't approach me quietly; he confronted me in public, saying, "It's none of your fucking business. If they want to do a business deal, it's none of your business. Butt out."

It's important to note that this all went down right

in front of where the black section watched TV. I had just returned from the weight room and was making my protein mix, so I went into my room to mix some powdered milk and water, seeing if he'd cool down. I was sitting on my bed, and he was right outside my room, still talking shit loudly.

When you are a prison section leader and you're in a situation like this, everybody watches you, looking for some sort of weakness. I had to make sure that everyone in all the sections knew that I wouldn't take shit. Because if I did, there would be no telling who would try something next.

I walked up to my door and told him, "Dude, I'm going to tell you one last time. *Shut the fuck up.*"

"Whatever. You're a pussy. You ain't going to do shit."

"All right." Instinct kicked in and I body slammed him, got into the mount position, and let his face have it with both fists.

The fight led to a lockdown. Guards rushed in, whistles blowing and screaming. I let Morlock up, and he was calling me crazy as he sulked off to his room for the lockdown. "You can call me crazy all you want," I said. "But what just happened is what anybody here would do."

I shut the door because everybody was locking down. By the time all 30 guards responded, all of us were already locked down in our rooms.

"Hey, you're looking for me," I yelled through the crack in the door. "I'm the reason why they called the PALS [Personal Alert System]. I was the one getting into a fight." They handcuffed me through my door and took me out, two guards on each side of me. They were making sure I wasn't going anywhere. When we got out of the pod, I said, "You guys can chill. I'm not going to do anything. It was just a personal thing between me and somebody else." As soon as I said that, three of them let go, but one of them kept holding on.

In the investigator's office, the watch commander said, "I've never seen you in here before. What's wrong? What happened?"

I shrugged my shoulders and said, "Morlock."

"Oh, well, that makes sense. I figured that was coming any day now." Everybody in the prison facility knew what kind of person Morlock was and that I was hopelessly trying to save him. No one thought it would work, and they were right.

I went down to solitary confinement for three days, the standard. While I was down there, the civilian staff members would come by one at a time and say stuff like "Good job, champ."

Morlock was hated universally by all the staff. He kept putting guards in jeopardy. Morlock was always reporting the guards and the staff members to the command. He was known as the guy who would snitch on anybody.

Still, they wanted him to remain my problem. They wanted to put him back in my housing unit.

"Not just no, but *hell* no," I said. "He does not have a place with me anymore."

I was the last person to give him a home. Once I made that decision, all the other white people made the same decision.

The black and Latino sections had long ago been burned by Morlock, and they universally refused to give him a home too.

With no place to go in general population, they had to send him to protective custody. There, he was off everybody's radar. It seemed to solve the Morlock problem, but I had one other guy to contend with: his mortal enemy.

Gibbs never forgave Morlock for testifying against

him in his court-martial. Gibbs had good reason to dislike Morlock. Being stabbed in the back by someone who doesn't have loyalty is something I understand well. I thought he might try to get even some day. Gibbs enjoyed being in solitary confinement anyway; he'd rather do his time there because he's a bookworm and he likes to just sit in his room and read.

With Morlock in protective custody, it took away the option of Gibbs getting even. Nobody could get to him in isolation. Gibbs approached me while I was walking on the rec field track. "L-T, did you put Morlock into protective custody?"

"Well, I don't want him, and nobody else wants him. Everybody they asked said no. So, yeah, that's on me."

"Well, I wish you hadn't done that," he said.

"Well, I'm sorry, man. It just happened. He wouldn't stop running his mouth."

Months later, I was lamenting to First Sergeant John Hatley, one of the other war crimes guys in there. "You know, I feel bad that I couldn't fix him." He grabbed me by the shoulder and turned me a little bit for emphasis. "Listen to what I'm about to tell you, youngster," he said. "You cannot fix him. Nobody can fix him. You gave it a good run for a couple of years, and I commend you for that. But don't waste your time on people like that. That man is morally corrupt."

MEDIA COVERAGE

Prison is all about daily routines. I would read my mail from two to four in the afternoon. Sean Hannity is on from two to five in Kansas City on AM radio, so I would listen to him in the background while I was going through letters. There were many occasions where I would tune in and hear him talking about me. That was really uplifting.

Hannity took up my case early on, as early as 2014. That gave Fox News host and former Guantanamo Bay guard Pete Hegseth a little bit of backup to make his own stand on the network airwaves.

I would be in the chow hall and somebody would come up to me and say, "Hey Clint, I saw you on Fox News" or "Hey Clint, I saw you on this" or "I heard you on this" or "I heard you on that." I wouldn't even know about it until they told me about it. This happened to me all the time.

Throughout the years, whenever there was any kind of significant media story about me, the guards would bring me in to the office and show me on the Internet. There was no other way for me to see the stories. Of course, we didn't have the Internet, and when Obama was the president, we only had CNN on the TV. When President Trump was elected in 2017, we got Fox News instead, and I was able to see more coverage.

There was a flurry of mainstream media attention in the spring of 2017 when my case wound through the courts. It wasn't going well at the Army Court of Criminal Appeals. I don't know why I was surprised. The judges on this court are Army lieutenant colonels. They know who butters their bread. In June, the Army judges denied my appeal.

The Court of Appeals for the Armed Forces, after a long wait, just flat out refused to even look at my case. No surprise there. The military would have had to admit they made a mistake in the first place. That would never happen.

There were no further legal fights. Few people realize that the Supreme Court can't get involved in most military cases because of an antiquated legal rule, as described in the following excerpt from a *New York Times* article[*]:

> Every defendant before an American criminal court today has a right to ask the highest court in the land to review his case—except members of the military. Every year, more than 1,000 are convicted of crimes in the military justice system. But because of a 1983 law, the Supreme Court cannot review most court-martial convictions—even in cases in which the defendant faces up to life in prison and has serious constitutional objections to his trial or sentence. The Reagan administration (which proposed the legislation) was worried that unlimited appeals from the military justice system would flood the justices' already overcrowded docket. But in 1988, Congress greatly reduced the number of appeals that the Supreme Court automatically had to hear.

I didn't expect much from the military justice system, so I was hardly even disappointed. However, a

[*] Eugene R. Fidell and Stephen I. Vladeck, "Second-Class Justice in the Military," *New York Times*, March 19, 2019.

bigger blow was about to land on me: Jimmy was about to be released.

He was scheduled to leave on my birthday, December 13. I was pissed, but he just said, "Dude, I don't control when I leave." Before he left, he gave me the following advice: "You tend to think the worst about people. Just remember that whenever you think somebody has disrespected you, before you gear up to fight, stop and think about it. Maybe they didn't really mean it. Maybe they were trying to say or do something else, and you took it the wrong way."

When he left, I was just kind of lost. Prison became more miserable after he left because I didn't really have anybody to talk to. I thought, *If my battle buddy's not here, I'm not going to be here either. I'm done with this place.*

In early 2019, I started to realize that John Maher was running out of steam. He had every right to because he'd been working for who knows how many hours every day for years trying to get me out. But nothing was working, and it was having a terrible psychological effect on him. He took my imprisonment to heart. I started to realize that maybe we needed to take another approach.

At a certain point, I decided to have another

attorney on my team, Don Brown, take the lead. Maher has an erudite personality, and Brown is more of a bulldog. He's an extremely aggressive trial attorney, the kind you would want in a fully contested criminal trial.

What I realized after watching a lot of Fox News and seeing the pardons that President Trump was granting was that the president respects being aggressive and assertive. He respects those qualities. I took all of this into account when I asked Don Brown to take the lead. He said "yes" with one condition: he wanted to keep Colonel Maher. It was a huge relief. Col. Maher is like a member of my family.

"That's absolutely fine with me," I said. "But I want *you* to be my mouthpiece."

In March 2019, at Maher's insistence, Brown published his book about my case, *Travesty of Justice: The Shocking Prosecution of Lt. Clint Lorance*. He laid out the case in intimate detail, highlighting how the Army did not permit the jury to consider evidence showing that Afghan National Army soldiers had fired first and how the Army kept biometric evidence from the jury.

Brown then set out to appear on every media outlet that he possibly could get on, doing what he does best, which is to go on the attack. He became the fierce media advocate I'd hoped he would be. He brought the fight to national television appearances and written opinion pieces. He pulled no punches. In one opinion piece for Fox News,[*] he quoted Phyllis Sisson, who wrote to him about the son she lost in Afghanistan in 2013: "Sir, I had a friend send me an excerpt from your book. It referenced an attack on June 3, 2013. One of the soldiers killed that day was my son 2LT Justin Sisson, 1-506th, 4BCT 1st PL A Co. I have followed LT Lorance's case. I strongly feel that the Obama Administration's policies contributed to my son's death."

Brown then brought the demand right to the White House: "What's really needed now to right a terrible wrong against Clint Lorance is intervention by President Trump, commander-in-chief of our armed forces. He needs to send a message loud and clear to all the men and women in the U.S. military stating that he has their backs on the battlefield."

Being a very calm, collected, polite attorney speaking legal-speak does not get President Trump's attention. He's passionate and he understands other people

---

[*] Don Brown, "President Trump, Please Free Army Lt. Clint Lorance, Unjustly Convicted of Murder in Afghanistan," Fox News, May 7, 2019.

who are passionate. You've got to speak the president's language if you're going to get his attention.

PARDONS AND RUMORS OF PARDONS

One thing I didn't have to worry about was the white section. I stepped down as leader on January 1, 2019, and made everyone aware of that date well ahead of time. All four of us in charge were supposed to go somewhere else around that time anyway. "I'm going to start transitioning out, so you guys start looking for somebody that you might like." I silently chose whom I wanted to take over a couple of weeks before I told anyone my plan to abdicate. He was a tough but mild-mannered red-haired Tennessee native who'd arrived after I'd taken over.

We had always thought that the president would pardon me and Governor Rod Blagojevich at the same time. He's the Democrat who would make all the Democrats happy, and I'm the Republican who would make the Republicans happy. Every time the president would talk about pardoning him, the lawyers would get excited, and everybody would get excited for me. (The former governor would be released in February 2020 along with a host of other figures from across the political spectrum.)

President Trump had known about me since 2016, but military pardons didn't become sexy until Eddie Gallagher's case got such attention. His wife is a marketing professional, so she got the word of his plight out there very effectively. Besides, everybody loves Navy SEALs. I think that's what brought the president's attention to it in earnest—when he had the opportunity to defend a Navy SEAL. I said, "You know what, the president *is* going to do this."

Months passed. The pins and needles didn't go away. I never lost faith in my president. Not for a moment.

COMING OUT VIA STARZ

In October 2019, the documentary *Leavenworth* on the STARZ network tackled my case. Paul Pawlowski, a veteran of sports broadcasts and documentaries, directed, with filmmaker Steven Soderbergh as an executive producer.

There was a lot of content that Paul gathered for that documentary that didn't make the final cut. I asked him why, and he said that the deal he made with the executive producer was that they could do the project as long as it did not tip the scale in either way, for me or for my opposition.

The first edit of the documentary was not neutral; it definitely favored me. Soderbergh asked for a re-edit, and they took out some of the more convincing stuff. The final cut of the documentary is pretty good, but the Don Brown book remains the absolute most comprehensive presentation of my case that exists today. I believe the documentary would have been more popular had they included *all* the evidence.

There was one part of the documentary that affected me directly. I had hidden my sexual orientation from everybody at Fort Leavenworth. But when *Leavenworth* came out in 2019, so did I. Everyone inside knew because their families saw it and told them about it.

Most of the inmates were actually supportive: "Hey,

just so you know, I think it's awesome. I think it's great. It doesn't change anything about the way I look at you." One guy came up to me and said, "I can't imagine the turmoil that you've had in your head this whole time. I respect you so much more now. You have my hundred percent support." I replied, "Well, thanks, bro." It was one of the most thoughtful things anyone has said to me.

I was the same exact person I was before they knew this, right? But, of course, after I was outed, I would be carrying something, and someone would say something like "Hey, I'll get that. I'll carry that for you." You know, like when you find out a friend is pregnant, and all of a sudden you want to help them do everything.

The main reason why some people don't come out is because they don't want to lose, in other people's eyes, what it means to be a man. It changes the way people see you. In mainstream culture, the only gay people we see are the people on *Will and Grace*. That show is hilarious, but it sets gay rights back decades because it makes people think that's the only kind of gay people out there. There are so many people who are in the closet, terrified to come out because they don't want to lose their masculinity. They don't want to lose what is associated with being a guy.

My celebrity created new annoyances. As always, I was in the gym every single day. After the documentary, a bunch of new people appeared in the gym, and every time I picked up a weight, someone would be there: "Hey man, do you need a spotter?"

"Seriously, do I look like I need a spotter? Besides, you don't even work out."

"Aw man, don't get offended."

Prisoners are opportunists. If they see any kind of opportunity open up, they will exploit it. They saw a guy in the media all the time, the president had even talked about him, and he's *gay*? Maybe I should go over there and try to make him fall for me. Most of these opportunists were straight guys. There were a few who would come up to me directly, "Hey man, are you seeing anybody right now?"

"Dude, I'm in prison. So are you. What's wrong with you?"

"Yeah, but you can do stuff here."

I think I said the phrase "Get the fuck away from me" a thousand times.

CONVERSATION WITH THE PRESIDENT

The excitement of Memorial Day weekend 2019 was only the beginning of a long, frustrating wait that was fed by snippets of news that nourished my hope for a presidential pardon. While the wait was difficult, my faith never wavered that in the end, Donald Trump would come through.

But that weekend was an emotional roller coaster. Sitting in my room, I packed up all my stuff and marked the packages with directions for where each should go. My whole family started converging on Fort Leavenworth, even my aunt and uncle who I hadn't seen in forever. On Memorial Day, my entire family was sitting in front of the TV listening for some word from the president.

Throughout the entire weekend, everybody in prison was telling me goodbye: "Bye Clint, take care. Make sure you fight for us. Don't forget about us." I didn't run across anybody who was mad; everybody was very excited. Everywhere I went, people said, "Thanks for everything you're doing here. Don't forget about us."

As Memorial Day passed without news, I became a ghost. People would see me in the chow hall and get depressed. It was like they were sharing in what I was experiencing, so it was weird. "Man, he's still here? The president must not give a shit about us after all." It was like I was at a funeral that Monday on Memorial Day; I was the last person in the world they wanted to see because they wanted to see me on TV leaving. People were openly coming up to me and saying, "I'm so sorry you're going through this bullshit. This is wrong. You should be out of here already."

"Dude, chill. It's all right," I told them. "It's going to happen. The president will do something."

As the delay stretched into the summer, something else was happening. The enormous support I had in so many quarters was steadily increasing.

During the months between Memorial Day and Veterans Day, my attorneys were aggressively market-ing my case in the media. This was all in an effort to show the president he had support for intervening in my case. We knew the White House was considering it because from time to time they would ask my attorneys for more information.

Finally, on November 4, 2019, Fox News host Pete Hegseth tweeted that he had personally spoken to the president and he was keen to pardon military prisoners before Veterans Day on November 11. So, again, I packed up my stuff; I had everything ready just in case and started living out of packed bags. I even had little signs on all the bags to the guards that read, "Turn this into laundry" or "Turn this into supply."

Life was a haze the week after Pete Hegseth's tweet. I knew that he was very close to the president and he would not have posted that tweet if he didn't know something. I knew it was going to happen. That certainty made those five days the most painful of my life in terms of emotional turmoil.

But Veterans Day came and went, still with no official word.

Then, on November 15, at about 3:45 in the afternoon, I was stretched out on my bunk listening to the Sean Hannity show. I had just been moved to minimum custody, so for the first time in six years, I was in a new pod and didn't really know anybody in there. I got a knock on my door, and there stood a sergeant first class, a man I had never seen before.

"I need you to come with me," he said. That's all he said to me.

He took me down the main hallway without telling me what was going on; I'm pretty sure he didn't know either. As I walked along, everybody was coming back from work. I was peppered with questions and comments: "Clint, are you gone? Are you gone? Are you leaving? See you! Bye, Clint." The whole prison had heard about the possible pardons, of course. I was able to tell at least 100 people goodbye as they walked by on their way back to their housing units. There were a lot of high fives.

But I did not know where we were going—or why. I hoped we were celebrating for a reason.

As we approached the main entrance of the facility, a civilian, Deputy Director of Operations Anthony Mendez, was waiting for us. "Hey, come with me," he said. "You've got a phone call."

"A phone call?"

He told the sergeant who was escorting me that he could leave, and one of the soldiers unlocked the door to the legal office. Mendez took me to an attorney/client consultation room in the back.

There was a tabletop speakerphone on the desk; a light on the phone started blinking and it made a weird little beep. The deputy director pushed the button on the phone, and a female voice identified herself as being from the Pentagon. She wanted to confirm that I was in the room.

"Yes ma'am," I said. "This is Clint."

"Okay, hang tight," she said. "Stay where you are. Keep this line open and stand by for senior defense officials."

A couple of minutes went by and Mendez and I were just looking at each other. I think he knew something was up and that's why he put himself on that detail because, really, the job should have gone to somebody with a more junior rank than he, but I think he wanted to handle it himself to make sure it got done right.

The phone started beeping again and Mendez answered it.

Another female voice came from the tabletop phone. She had a real country accent. "Clint Lorance?"

"Yes, ma'am."

"Okay, stand by for the president."

Immediately when she said that, Mendez took out a little pocket notebook and got ready to write notes down. He also logged the time the call started.

President Trump came on the line. "Hello?"

"Hello, Mr. President. This is Lieutenant Clint Lorance."

"Clint, it's good to hear from you," he said. "Here in 10 minutes...well, here in about two minutes, I'm going to sign a full pardon and expungement of your record. It will be like it never happened."

Then he chuckled and said, "Hell, your record will probably be cleaner than mine."

Should I laugh with the president? I didn't know.

Then he said, "Clint, in this room, we got the vice president. Say hi, Mike."

The vice president said something along the lines of "Lieutenant, I just want you to know that we've supported you for a long time. This should have never happened to you and we're going to make this right." The vice president seemed like a really disciplined guy; he said "Lieutenant" every time he addressed me.

"Well, thank you, sir."

Then the president asked, "How have you been treated?"

"The American people can be assured that their military prisoners are treated with dignity and respect," I said, or something like that.

This was becoming a conversation, and I felt comfortable talking with President Trump directly. I had something I wanted to tell him. "Sir, I know that with the Chelsea Manning thing with President Obama, when Chelsea was let out of prison by the president, she went out and started talking crap about him."

He interjected, "Yeah, that was really something wasn't it? If it would have been me, I would have thrown her back in there. Well, he/she, whatever it is."

"Sir, I just want to let you know that I speak for my entire family when I say that would never happen in a million years," I continued. "We understand loyalty where I'm from, and we will always be 100 percent loyal to you, and that extends to you as well, Mr. Vice President."

"Well, what are you going to do now?" Trump asked.

"Well, sir, I don't know. I'm thinking about going to law school."

He replied, "Okay, well, good luck." The call ended after well-wishing all around. The director of operations timed it; he said I was on the phone for about 11 minutes.

I was a free man—almost.

The prison staff were ready to release me as soon

as the president ordered it. They parked me at the secondary entrance, at the back of the prison. The deputy director of operations, Mr. Mendez, waited with me there for all six hours. He ordered some soldiers to go to my room and get my belongings.

"Look, all of my stuff's already bagged up. Just go read the notes on them." After a while, word came back that the room was empty. "Thanks for the notes," the guards said. "That was so easy." I love it when a good plan comes together.

Later, a master sergeant walked in with my uniform in his hands, the one Ross Creel safeguarded and delivered to my family. Lt. Col. Bull Gurfein from the United American Patriots brought it for me to change into.

I sat there in my uniform for about five hours. They were the best, sweetest, most amazing hours of my life—sitting there in the intake room. Six years earlier, I had come into that same room in my PTs. That's where they strip-searched me and gave me my prison uniform. Now I was sitting there in my full dress uniform, waiting on my ride to leave.

I just sat there, doing absolutely nothing. It was amazing. I think I needed that time. What I didn't know was that, at that moment, people on my team were fighting to get me released that night and not the following Monday.

I cannot tell you how rewarding it was to be able to walk into that place in my PT uniform and walk out of that place in my dress uniform. I'll never forget that moment. It was just so, *Holy crap, this is over!* I don't know. It's as if it assigned a certain meaning to my time there and made it all worthwhile. It almost felt like I had completed a mission and now I was done with the Army. I was going to be a civilian. And I am completely done with the Army. I'm going to move on with my life.

I came out of the front gates. Leavenworth releases prisoners in a parking lot. They can't release them on post, they have to release them off post, so they take them to the nearest parking lot off post. As soon as you exit the front gate, there's a parking lot immediately to the right. So the prison van stopped right there, and I got out. Colonel Gurfein was there with Colonel Maher and Terry Buckler, driving a white Chevy Tahoe. They put me in the Tahoe and drove me across the street to a really nice hotel.

That's where I first saw my family. I saw my cousin Jamie, Aunt Jean, Uncle Brian, and all the kids; they were standing at the front door, bouncing up and down like crazy. There were random people I didn't know standing around, onlookers wondering what was going on. After I hugged everybody I knew, we walked into the lobby.

In the military, you're always moving forward. You don't just stop somewhere and smell the roses; you're always moving toward an objective. As soon as I got out of the vehicle, my mind made the next objective that hotel lobby.

Nobody had planned on me getting a pardon late on Friday night, so no one had rented a hotel room for that night. They were all supposed to be checked out and gone. We went into the lobby, where a bunch of pizzas were laid out. They had decorated the lobby, a really ad hoc decorating job, and it was perfect.

Some people were there just because they were staying at the hotel, but the crowd mostly consisted of a small handful of my family. Terry Buckler came over and handed me his phone. Colonel Allen West was on the phone. The colonel welcomed me home and said that he'd been fighting for me for a long time. I thought it was great that I finally got to talk to him on the phone. He'd been a personal hero and source of strength for me for a long time.

After we ate and celebrated, it was midnight. I

needed the next objective. We couldn't just sit in the lobby all night. Col. Gurfein rented a couple of rooms for us, and we racked out for the night.

The first order of business the next day was to thank the president publicly. Out of loyalty, I demanded that Fox News get my first interview. The UAP staff started making calls. They suggested getting me home for a welcome home ceremony there. On Sunday, they'd fly me out to New York so that first thing Monday morning I could do my first interview on *Fox & Friends*.

There were a bunch of people already contacting my lawyers about interviews. All of the mainstream media outlets wanted to interview me, but I told them all no. I basically issued a standing directive to my team saying, "If you interview with them, I'm not going to endorse it." I knew that they were only trying to use me in some way against the president. I would not hurt the president in any way or be a party to it. Period.

While I was in New York, Jen Berrios reached out via Facebook. "I want to come see you." She got on a train and came down to the city. We went out to a Korean restaurant, and we stayed out really late, which made me feel terrible because she had to be at work the next day, but I was so happy to spend time with her.

We caught up. I found out that there had been a disagreement between Jen and her partner about whether or not to keep the baby. Eventually, the disagreement led to separation. Jen moved up to New York with the child after she graduated college. She lives just outside of Albany and works with the state auditor's office. God help the state organizations in New York when they misuse their funds because she *will* find out.

In New York, she met a sergeant first class in the Army and ROTC instructor. Berrios married her, and in 2019, they had a healthy baby boy.

I loved seeing Jen again. It was like we had never missed a beat. Army buddies are like that. You can unplug from one another's life and then plug right back in.

AFTER THE HURRICANE

I have a notebook from Fort Leavenworth that has "Post-Release Plans" written on the outside of it. Inside are all these detailed plans of what I was going to do when I left prison. There are four chapters: Reintegration, Homestead, Family Planning, and Politics.

It's very detailed on exactly what I had to do: redirect mail and all of the publication subscriptions, listed by title; get a cell phone with a specific carrier and plan; get a driver's license; buy a cheap truck.

I didn't open the notebook after I got out of Leavenworth, but looking at it now, I can see that I followed it step by step. I went back to Texas and bought an F-150. I got a phone, my license, a job, and an apartment. I took the Law School Admission Test. I'm applying to law schools. I'm rebuilding myself.

It really was a struggle at first. I felt directionless, broke, and unmarketable. Despite having the pardon, my status is the equivalent of a dishonorable discharge, and I have a criminal record. Even though it has been officially forgiven by the pardon, the crime is still on my record, and I must tell people about it and check that box on applications. But I am not in prison.

My cousin Jamie highlighted something for me on the phone. She said, "You were more squared away and you had your stuff together more when you were in Leavenworth."

"Well, thanks a lot."

"I think the reason why is because you were just kind of sprung out of there all of a sudden. Most people that leave have a couple of months to prepare. You've been kind of directionless. Somebody spun you around and you've just been going in all these different directions."

She was right. I didn't see it until somebody pointed it out. The only hiccup in my notebook plan was that I had been pardoned and not paroled. That's why I foundered a little bit; I didn't know I was leaving that day.

What a great problem to have.

Something else weighed on me. My whole life, I've been trying to be independent on my own and just do my own thing. And now that I'm a civilian, I miss the military. Thankfully, I'm in the civilian world, but I even miss Leavenworth because military prison is still the military.

I miss being able to go right next door and knock on the door to talk to somebody who thinks just like me, who has been through the same thing I've been through, and who understands exactly where I'm coming from. Embry-Riddle is a really great school in the town where I live, but I have nothing in common with all the kids who attend.

A lot of veterans are struggling, and I think that's a big reason why it is extremely hard for them to connect with the civilian population. Out of the military, to put it simply, they have lost the brotherhood.

The transition to the civilian world is insane. I thought I was a pretty smart guy and I'm pretty adaptable. I would always read about military veterans having issues when they left the military, but I just didn't realize the huge difference between military and civilian life.

Democrats and Republicans, the American people as a whole, they're just amazing. They love the military. They'll come up to you and thank you for your service, but they have no idea what they're thanking you for. I think that's a reason why a lot of military people choose law enforcement or firefighting as a second career. They miss the brotherhood and you get those when you're in law enforcement.

I've actually thought about being a cop, and I was recently offered a job as a state game warden. I don't think I could do that with my record, but for that brief moment, the idea of having brothers and sisters again, of being part of a team again, warmed my soul.

After my release, there was a whirlwind of events and appearances. One day, Justin Lyle saw a United American Patriots event announced on Facebook and he just showed up at the hotel in Las Vegas. One of the volunteers came up to me: "Hey, there's somebody here who wants to see you. I don't know if you know him or not. Is it okay? His name is Justin Lyle."

"Hell yeah."

We just plugged right back in. We hadn't seen each other in 15 years, but we know each other so well that it was like we were together yesterday. Bonds like that are hard to find in the civilian world.

UNPACKING AN INTERRUPTED LIFE

I'm reconnecting with all my stuff that is familiar to me. I think it may be the final part of the healing process in terms of getting back to being a whole person again, at least being who I was before.

I still have all my uniforms and a big box of old military stuff that I'm not going to have any use for ever again. My family turned in four or five big crates of gear back to the Army, but some stuff they just don't want back. After staying in a storage container, the kneepads are moldy and the gear is dusty. I had all the medals for my uniform in a little plastic case and when I opened it up, it was weird to see rust on them.

I drove back from Texas with boxes of books that I mailed back to my parents from prison. Now I have a great collection of every book I read while I was in Leavenworth. The collection includes volumes about Vietnam. I've just had to stack them up in my apartment like in an old bookstore.

In the news, there is discussion of a drawdown in Afghanistan and peace talks with the Taliban. I think it's absolutely genius that the Trump administration went directly around the Afghan government to do the 2020 peace deal. At the end of the day, the Taliban's pulling the strings in that country. It doesn't matter who the president of Afghanistan is, the Taliban is really in control.

I know that we went over there as a reaction to 9/11, but I'm not sure we still need to be there after almost two decades. The Obama administration was allowing the enemy to outmaneuver us at every juncture. You need to have some academics in every administration, but you also need people with real-world experience. We lost the war for the entire eight years that Obama

was commander-in-chief because of the way his administration micromanaged the fighting.

I'm not sure that we're winning it now, either, but
at least we're able to fight. At the end of the day, the
Taliban and Al-Qaeda and all the people we fight there
do not play by the rules. They are smart enough to
use our rules against us. We should absolutely follow
the Geneva Convention, but we shouldn't make up our
own stupid rules on top of that to make it harder. That's
what happened under the Obama administration.

We are engaged in nation-building in a place that
has no aspiration to be a nation. It has no infrastruc-
ture and no real crops to offer, except for opium. When
you have a vice president who's a warlord himself, there
is something wrong with the country. I think the best
that we can possibly do is to try to deal with them so we
can get what we need out of their broken society, which
is to never let 9/11 happen again.

There is the argument that we either fight them in
Kandahar or we fight them in Kansas City, and I agree
with that. I think we need to still have a presence of
some sort. But I think we can project power in much
smarter ways.

In my opinion, conventional forces don't belong in

Afghanistan. If we had some CIA and Special Forces assets on a small scale, we might be just as successful as what we're doing now. It's just not a "big military" fight. I think we could save a lot of money by bringing people back to the United States and putting that money into Homeland Security and law enforcement to make sure 9/11 doesn't happen again.

POLITICAL VOICE

I have jumped ahead like a time traveler between 2013 and 2019, and I'm shocked at how nasty people are willing to be to one another online now. It wasn't like that back in 2013.

Every day, people I engage with online will discount anything I say because I support President Trump.

I was recently arguing online with a guy with a degree from the Wharton Business School at University of Pennsylvania. I speak to everybody in a respectful way, but this guy ended up admitting, "Well, to be honest with you, you've got to be an idiot because you support Trump. Anybody that supports Trump's an idiot."

"I expected more coming from an Ivy League graduate, to be honest with you," I replied. "I expected you to at least be able to hold an argument and a debate and talk about issues and not just 'I hate Trump so you must be stupid because you're on his team.'"

It's important to remind people that we want to be able to disagree. I wouldn't want to live in a society like China or North Korea, where there is an official body that tells you what to believe. I want arguments between Democrats and Republicans. Many people online say things like "Get rid of Democrats. Vote them all out." Why would you ever want one party? You've got to have dissension. You've got to have people checking each other and balancing things out. It's always a zero-sum, all-or-nothing kind of proposal. It makes no sense to me.

I'm shocked that people don't understand why I support President Trump. The guy literally saved my life. If the guy rescued me from drowning in a lake, I would have the same degree of loyalty to him. It's a huge deal to be a president of the United States going down in history books for helping somebody who is branded a war criminal. I think that makes me even more loyal to him because he put so much on the line to help me.

Not supporting the president would mean shutting

up; deleting my Instagram, Parler, Twitter, and Facebook accounts; and forgetting about politics. But I won't do that. Right now, I fight for him online in my spare time. I try to logically reason with people and point out certain things from my experiences.

I would never in a million years say anything bad about him. I'm just so shocked that people don't understand that. One night, someone asked me, "What's your angle? What are you gunning for? Do you want a position at the White House?"

"No, dude. I'm just loyal."

I always try to build bridges. I have a new mission to consider, and I'll need all the support I can get from every quarter in order to get it done. My purpose is nothing less than fixing the military justice system.

NEW MISSION

What happened to me will happen, and in some cases is already happening, to someone else. When the United States decides to send somebody to prison for something that happens in war, they do it based on politics.

It's a brute calculation: What can they gain from that imprisonment?

If there is no conversation about war crimes, if there is no argument between our negotiators, soldiers won't be going to prison. But the United States has military personnel in more than 130 countries. When they need an example, they can always find one. You are government property, and if you are needed to be used as a bargaining chip as I was, if you are needed to make some general officer's career, then you will be.

I am definitely going to law school, and I definitely want to help reform the military justice system. There are certain things that I realize are wrong with the system, and these things allow for someone who is wrongfully convicted to stay in prison and not have a chance. There are certain flaws that other jurisdictions in this country, at state and federal levels, have already reformed and fixed that have just been ignored in the military justice system, and we need to fix those.

There needs to be a military district attorney. Currently, the person who decides if somebody should go to court-martial is the commanding general. Just because someone has been in the Army for 30 or 40 years does not mean that he or she is qualified to determine whether somebody is a criminal. What qualifies someone is a professional legal education.

There's been a lot of pushback in terms of whether the military should relinquish that system in the interest of justice. It's a balance between the discipline of the military and justice generally. The order and discipline of the military demand that the generals and the admirals always maintain control over the military justice system. They use the military justice system as a tool to ensure that the force remains disciplined, and I don't disagree with them completely.

Here's why. You can have a senator like Kirsten Gillibrand of New York, who is complaining all the time about what she calls a sexual assault epidemic in the military. When she gets enough people to support that in Congress, they start exerting pressure to make the Pentagon jump to their concerns. Since they control the purse strings, they can call the shots.

On the flip side, general officers and admirals have to be confirmed by the Senate to be promoted. Once you're a one star, you want to be a four star. And you may one day face a U.S. senator telling you that they are not going to support your promotion because they don't think you're hard enough on sexual assault.

For example, President Obama went to Honolulu and made an announcement that we've got to bring the hammer down in the military whenever somebody is accused of sexual assault. After that pronouncement, Leavenworth was bursting at the seams with people who were convicted of sexual assault. It's not because more people were sexually assaulting other soldiers; it's because more senior officers were trying to make Congress and the Department of Defense happy.

The military justice system is used in many ways for self-gain, and that's one of them. As a result, there are many people sitting in military jails around the world right now who are not guilty but who were put there because an officer, general, or admiral wanted to make Senator Gillibrand or some other member of Congress happy. I know it sounds like a conspiracy, but I've seen it firsthand.

I found my next objective by tapping into the person who I was before Leavenworth and the person I became while I was inside. My role now is what it always was: to fight for warriors. That's what I did while I was in combat. My job was to fight for the fighters, to advocate for my warriors.

That's what I need to do now, but I need to prepare

for the fight of a lifetime. It's important that I go to law school. Whenever anybody asks why I want to be a lawyer, I tell them, "I want to try to get people out of prison who don't belong there."

I'm still putting one foot in front of the other, heading for the objectives ahead.

EPILOGUE

AS SOON AS I WAS RELEASED from prison, I went on a thank you tour in the media. Most of the interviews were in Washington, D.C., and New York. That only lasted a few weeks. In December, a friend of mine, Wendell DallaRosa, a retired special operations senior NCO, invited me to move to Florida. I needed to be truly free, and I knew that if I stayed in Texas, I would get bogged down trying to solve all of my family's problems. So I took him up on it and moved to Central

Florida, near Daytona Beach. I fit right in here; it is Trump Country.

Let me be very clear here, I am and always will be appreciative of President Donald Trump. Although the president said to me on the phone that "it would be like it never happened" and my "record will be expunged," those who work in the Pentagon and Department of Justice (DOJ) must have had other ideas. I received a memo from the DOJ saying that I still have a criminal record and I still need to disclose it to anyone who asks, but that I was granted "official forgiveness."

So, essentially, I am again able to vote, run for office, and buy guns, but only as long as I present my presidential pardon paperwork. I presented the paperwork when applying to apartment complexes in Florida and was turned down by dozens. It was only when I applied to an apartment complex that was owned by Trump supporters that I was accepted.

Most people are surprised to hear that I was not given any back pay from the Army. I still have a "dismissal" from the Army, which is the same thing as a dishonorable discharge.

One of the most challenging parts of applying to law schools has been explaining all of this.

EPILOGUE

So, here I am, starting over from square one. Jamie says it's like I'm 18 years old again. One thing is for sure, I have my freedom. It's not without considerable challenges, but I am free. And for that, I thank God and President Trump.

END

ACKNOWLEDGMENTS

I'd like to dedicate this book to the men and women who have been wrongly convicted in military courts. There are many of you, and only you and your family know the true nature of the Uniform Code of Military Justice. It is in your honor that I fight.

Thank you to my incredible family, who never stopped believing in me. Each and every one of you embodies the true meaning of love and loyalty. To be a part of such a wonderful family is truly unique and incredible. I love you all.

To my agent Ian Kleinert, thank you for believing in me and patiently dealing with me throughout this process. I know I can be demanding and difficult to deal with at times. You're an incredible guy.

To editor Kate Hartson, thank you for giving me a chance and for your consistent, compassionate, articulate, structured, and vigilant leadership. You lead an incredibly talented team.

To my writing partner Joe Pappalardo, thank you

for making sense of my chaotic stories and for your patient deliberation.

To Lieutenant Colonel Bull Gurfein (USMC), Major Bill Donahue (USMC), Ms. Elizabeth Brown, and the team at United American Patriots, thank you for fighting for me when it was not popular and when no one else would. You are a world-class organization. And because you believe in fighting for justice for our military and law enforcement, I will support you each and every day of the rest of my life.

To Professor Don J. Snyder, thank you for your incredible lifetime of caring and writing books and movies about the human side of it all and the effects our treatment of one another has on humanity.

To my friend Dick McDermott, thank you for empowering the team from the background and for teaching me so much about what it means to be a leader in today's complex and litigious world. You are a class act, sir. Much love and respect.

To my absolutely brilliant legal team. Renowned author, former US Navy Commander, and attorney Don Brown; former US Army JAG attorney Kevin Mikolashek; retired US Air Force JAG attorney Lt. Col. Dave Bolgiano; attorneys Christopher Joseph, Dianne

Bellquist, and Carrie Parker, and the team at Joseph, Hollander, and Craft in Topeka; and retired New York Police Department (NYPD) Sergeant and lead investigator Bill "Coach" Carney. Thank you all.

A special thanks to retired US Army Lieutenant Colonel John N. Maher. You are exactly the kind of lawyer I want to be. Your dedication to justice and our legal system is nothing short of extraordinary. You are a true friend and mentor.

To author Lynn Vincent and my fellow Army brother Captain Roger Hill, thank you for exposing the military's broken processes and systems.

To retired US Army Ranger, Paratrooper, and Command Sergeant Major Daniel Gustafson, 82nd Airborne Division, thank you for being what a leader should be. Unfortunately, I don't think they make leaders like you anymore. You have true backbone, strength of character, and the willingness to stand up to the brass when they're wrong. You're a true inspiration to paratroopers everywhere.

And to all of the people out there who tell me "no" or "you can't do that" or "you're a terrible person, you'll never succeed," thank you. Keep it up. You motivate me.

ACKNOWLEDGMENTS

I could write an entire book about all of great people who have made this book possible and have changed my life. To be sure, we don't fight any war alone. To all of you out there, I love you, and let's keep moving forward. God bless you.